TRA͡ DUSSLES

Or, Foods for Wars, Peace, And Potlucks

2nd Edition

a book by
Siobhan Medhbh O'Roarke
&
Cordelia Toser

Preface to the second edition

Preface to the second edition

Many old dogs need to learn a bunch of new tricks, and I was one of them. In the nine years since I've moved to the West Kingdom, I've been humbled by the talents I've found, and been privileged to learn from many of them. Chief among them must be *Crystal of the Westermark*, who was my apprentice for all of about 10 hours before the Crown offered her the accolade of the Laurel, and her fellow apprentice *Cynthia du Pre Argent*, who was and is friend and family, taught me more than I ever could have taught her. I'm thrilled that both of these ladies have been recognized and rewarded by our Society for their talents. My area of learning, while long on execution (things *did* taste good) was seriously deficient in depth of period sources, and Crystal and Cynthia have opened many doors for me. The other cooks in the West, whose names I'm not going to try to remember because I'll forget someone, have excited me with their enjoyment of food, cooking, and each other. It certainly keeps me from being bored.

The Shire of Crosston is my new heart's home in the West, and thank goodness they like to eat! Next time they do an *Iron Chef meets Mooseland* contest, I'm there! I especially appreciate being kept on my toes by *Elspeth, Rafael, Allessandro, Collette, John Theophilous,* and my consort, *Aaron of Buckminster*. And my constant amazement goes to those folk who have turned out to be kitchen help for events that were not even in their backyards: *Duncan, Geoffroi, Birgitta, Catherine, Hilary, Crystal, Siobhan f, Piper, Eilis, Thomas, Sean, Keegan, Valgard, Lee, Meg, Geoffrey Matt, Flidais, John (*do all Aussies make great piecrust?*)*...I hadn't realized what a huge crew they were until I started listing them out. No wonder my feasts go so well! This listing doesn't even begin to mention the many gentlemen, royal and noble alike, who have made cleanup afterward a feast for the eyes — you haven't lived until you've seen a septet of Western knights, stripped to the waist, singing bawdy Elizabethan songs while they wash dishes.... And let us not forget to count those folks who aren't in the SCA and still show up to help run the kitchen — *Jen, Michael, Sydney, Hannah, Martin the Pirate, Caitlin,* and *Elton*.

My deepest thanks go to *Cordelia Toser*, without whom you would not be holding this book in your hands. By my own negligence I ended up with source files for this book that could no longer be opened by any of the software I had available. Cordelia hand-typed the book in from her copy of the first edition, added in all the new recipes, made corrections, and looked at it with fresh eyes. I was glad to count her as my friend before. Now I'm very happy to introduce her as co-author of this book.

But most of all, I thank you, our readers. I get so excited when you come to me to tell me about the dishes you've tried, or that your household or group now thinks of some dish as *your* specialty. Please, keep telling me about your new triumphs.

Siobhan Medhbh O'Roarke
Way East Crosston, Cynagua,
The West

Pat McGregor
Cameron Park, CA
email: pat@elfhill.com
July, 2002

Another preface to the second edition

I wanted to cook before I was tall enough to see what was on the kitchen counter, but my mother would not let me try cooking on my own until I was 10. At that age, the prospect of cleaning up the kitchen afterward almost ended my cooking career right then and there! My godmother was a schoolteacher who did part-time catering in the afternoons. I spent many hours watching her make mayonnaise from scratch, petit fours, and assemble wonderfully decorated 3-tiered wedding cakes after she'd made all the sugar roses by hand. The basis for my love of cooking, and any culinary skill I might possess, are from their teachings and enjoyment of food once prepared.

It was *Wulfric of Creigull* and *Juturna the Musical* who first dragged me into an SCA feast kitchen about ten years ago, and I haven't looked back. The prospect of actually reading and redacting original recipes from non-modern-English sources was daunting at first, but with the encouragement of people like *Crystal of the Westermark, Siobhan Medhbh, Juana Isabella, Cariadoc of the Bow* and *Elizabeth of Dendermonde*, I've gotten confident at doing just that. I feel that I now do a pretty good job of preparing a period dish without trying to turn it into a modern one. I've recently become addicted to looking through "period" cookbooks when planning a dinner for unsuspecting dinner guests.

My great thanks go to *Siobhan Medhbh O'Roarke*, who was kind enough to ask me if I'd be interested in doing a bit of typing for her. As you see, the project grew into a lot more than that for me. It was a great pleasure for me to be involved in making this cookbooklet a little bit better, and I hope it brings some pleasure to your life as well.

Cordelia Toser
Crosston East, Mists,
The West

Carole Newson-Smith
Hayward, CA
email: cordeliatoser@hotmail.com
July, 2002

Acknowledgments

Learning to cook medievally requires not only a kitchen and some idea of how to follow a recipe, but teachers, guinea pigs, and fellow researchers.

My thanks and gratitude go to *Duchess Caellyn FitzHugh* of the Middle, who was my first teacher in medieval food. *Caellyn* introduced me to surviving period sources, and taught me the science of feeding 400 people and the art of creating an environment where they would enjoy it. She and *Jeahanne de St. Brieuc* encouraged me to have fun at the same time. The hordes of folks who have worked in my kitchens and as servers for my events helped me figure out what "easy-to-follow" really means.

Carlo, Myrra, Aldric, 'A'isha, Graidhne, Charles, Melisande, Eliahu, Cordelia, John, Lisa, Beorthwine, Dulciñea, Robert, Guillame, Dag, Juaña, Robyyan, Megan, Gwydion, Daffyd, and many others have eaten my trials, given me hints, pointers, practical and constructive criticism, and friendship. Palymar, Osion, and Kay not only provided all of the above, but taught me how to use modern sanitary practices to avoid giving everyone food poisoning or worse.

Cariadoc, Elizabeth, and *Katerine* have helped me learn more about history, research, and sources. What treasures they are! *Katerine* provided many useful suggestions and research findings, as well as much bibliographic information. *Tibor* collected the SCA merchant information.

Alfred, Siobhan fidhlair, and *Wander* have helped me find ways to translate my knowledge into the culture of the West kingdom. *Siobhan* also provided some of the recipes. Northwoods, Cynnabar, Crosston, and Mountain's Gate have taste-tested many of the recipes in this booklet.

The online community of **rec.food.historic** gave me much food for thought, as well as excellent source material and hints to find more cookbooks and sources than I'll ever read through.

Ellisif, Michael Fenwick, Edward ("Wood Guy"), Cynthia, and *Gwenhyfaer* proofread and made intelligent suggestions. *Malcolm MacPherson* and his lady *Kaitlin* threatened me with dire punishment if I did not publish this pamphlet, and the writing of it has been as useful for me as I hope the pamphlet is for you. *Kaitlin,* in addition, did all the lovely pen and ink drawings scattered throughout the book, as well as the cover art.

Lastly, I salute my sister *Gwyneth Felton* and her cooking partner *Serena Homes,* gracious and accomplished cooks who, like me, perpetually fear that there will not be enough food.

As always, the good things about this publication are due to these contributors; any errors are strictly my own fault.

Siobhan Medhbh O'Roarke
Mountain's Gate, Cynagua,
The West

Pat McGregor
Cameron Park, CA
June 1996

Acknowledgments

Acknowledgments

This book is dedicated to two kinds of people:
Those who love to experiment and try new foods,
and those who love them enough to eat whatever turns out.

Acknowledgments

Table of Contents

Preface to the second edition	**3**
Another preface to the second edition	**4**
Acknowledgments	**5**
Errata List	**15**
Bringing the Middle Ages to the Potluck	**16**
Not the Enchanted Ground	*16*
Vegetarians	*17*
Food Tables	**19**
What to Serve	**22**
No Cook Choices	*22*
Minimal Cook Foods	*23*
Adventures in Medieval Cooking	*25*
Coping with Camping Technology	*25*
Stews & Soups	*25*
Meats & Sauces	*25*
Cold Pies	*25*
Salads & Vegetables	*26*
Refrigeration, Food Management, & Relaxation	*26*
Emergency Rations	**28**
Where to find it	**29**
Large SCA Events	*29*
Local Non-Supermarket Sources	*30*
Natural food co-ops	*30*
Shop-by-Mail	*31*
Making Do	**34**
Recipes	**36**
Common Items	**37**
❖ *Powder Douce*	*37*
❖ *Powder Forte*	*38*
❖ *Almond Milk*	*39*
❖ *Breadcrumbs*	*40*
❖ *Paste (Flaky Pie Crust)*	*41*
❖ *A Coffin*	*42*
❖ *Verjuice*	*44*
Sauces	**45**
❖ *Sage Sauce*	*45*
❖ *Sawse Cameline (Cinnamon Sauce)*	*46*
❖ *Garlek Cameline (Garlic Cinnamon Sauce)*	*47*
❖ *Cormarye (Caraway Sauce for Pork)*	*48*

❖ Jance Sawse (Walnut Garlic Sauce)	49
❖ Piper Sauce (Pepper Sauce)	50
❖ Sawse Gauncile (Garlic Sauce)	51
❖ Verde Sawse (Green Sauce)	52

Savory Pies   54

❖ Braun Pye (Pork Pie)	54
❖ Pyes of Chiken (Chicken Pie)	56
❖ Grete Pye (Beef, Chicken, & Hard Boiled Egg Pie)	57
❖ Pygge in a Coffin (Ham Pie)	58
❖ Auter Tartus (Tart of Cheese)	60
❖ How to make Tartes of Spinage	61
❖ Tart de Bry (Brie Tart)	62
❖ To Make a Tarte of Spinnage (Spinach Pie)	63

Fruits   64

❖ Chardewardon (Pear Sauce)	64
❖ Bolas/Bullace/Bullyce (Dark Plums)	65

Vegetables   66

❖ Salat (Green Salad)	67
❖ Rape Armate (Turnip Cake, or Armoured Turnips)	68
❖ Caboches in Potage (Cabbage in Broth)	69
❖ Funges (Mushrooms)	70
❖ A Grand Sallet of Beets, Currants & Greens	71
❖ Cress in Lent with Milk of Almonds	72
❖ A dysshe of Artichokes (Baked Artichokes)	73
❖ Benes y-Fride (Fried Beans)	74
❖ Frumenty (Wheat & Milk Pottage)	75
❖ Mustard Greens	76
❖ Buttered Marrows	77
❖ Butterd Worts (Buttered Greens)	78

Cheese & Eggs   80

❖ Loseyns (Cheese Lasagne)	80
❖ Stuffed Tubes (Fried Cheese)	82
❖ Longe Frutours (Fried Fresh Cheese)	83
❖ An Herbal Dish or Two of Eggs (Herbed Omelette)	84

Fish   86

❖ Salmon Roste in Sauce	86

Poultry & Rabbit   88

❖ Sawse Madam (Goose [or Chicken] with Fruit Stuffing)	88
❖ Chike Endored (Gilded Chicken)	89
❖ Viaunde of Cypres Ryalle (Chicken in Sweet Sauce)	90
❖ Hotchpot de Poullaine (Chicken Casserole)	91
❖ Two Chikens from One (Stuffed Chicken)	92
❖ Conejas (Grilled Rabbit)	94

Acknowledgments

❖ *White Tharidah of Al-Rashid (Chicken Stew)* — 96
❖ *A Recipe for a Dish of Chicken* — 98

Meat — 100

❖ *Yrchouns (Sausage Hedgehogs)* — 100
❖ *Stewed Beeff (Braised/Stewed Beef)* — 102
❖ *Bor in Counfett (Ham Slices in Honey Glaze)* — 103
❖ *For to make Alawder de beef (Stuffed Beef Rolls)* — 104
❖ *Bourbelier of Fresh Boar (Roast Pork)* — 105
❖ *Braun en Peurade (Pork in Pepper Sauce)* — 106
❖ *Civé de Veel (Veal Stew)* — 108
❖ *Mortrews Blank (Chicken & Pork Hash)* — 110
❖ *Stekys of Venson or Bef (Venison or Beef Steaks)* — 111
❖ *Poumes (Meatball Apples)* — 112

Soups — 114

❖ *Roo Broth (Venison Soup)* — 114
❖ *Sowpys Dorre (Onions on Toast)* — 115
❖ *Green Broth of Eggs & Cheese Soup* — 116
❖ *Jowtes of Almand Mylke (Green Almond Soup)* — 117
❖ *Salomene (Fish Soup)* — 118

Beverages — 120

❖ *Sekanjabin (Oxymel)* — 120
❖ *Cordials* — 122
❖ *To Make The Surfit Water (Dried Fruit Cordial)* — 122
❖ *To Make Raspberry Wine (Fresh Fruit Cordial)* — 123

Desserts — 124

❖ *Wardonys in Syryp (Pears in Wine Syrup)* — 124
❖ *Strawberye (Strawberry Pudding)* — 126
❖ *Creme Boyled (Custard Pudding)* — 128
❖ *Daryoles (Custard Tart)* — 129
❖ *Per Fare Tortiglione Ripieno* — 130
(Yeast Cake Stuffed with Raisins) — 130
❖ *Erbowle (Fresh Plum Pudding)* — 133
❖ *Quaking Pudding (Batter Pudding)* — 134
❖ *Orange-Butter Sauce* — 135
❖ *A Flaune of Almayne (Mixed Fruit Pie)* — 136
❖ *A Tart of Almonds (Almond Pie)* — 137
❖ *Cryspes (Sweet Fried Dough)* — 138
❖ *A Fruit Pudding (Steamed Suet Pudding)* — 140

Menus — 142

Feast for Christmas Day — 142
Menu Planning Help Online — 144
Sample Menus — 145
Golden Rivers Anniversary Feast 2000 — 145

Not the Enchanted Ground   Traveling Dysshes

A Twelfth Night Feast for the American Recorder Society	*146*
Scottish Night Feast at Collegium Occidentalis, Fall 1999	*147*
Collett & Alessandro's Wedding	*148*
Jingles Feast 1995	*149*

Sources — 150
Books & Websites with Modern Recipes	*150*
Sources with Only Medieval Recipes	*154*
Books about Food & Cooking	*156*

Recipes Removed from the first edition — 157
❖ *Braun (Roast Pork in Dry Marinade)*	*157*
❖ *Mincemeat Tart*	*158*
❖ *Brandy Hard Sauce*	*158*
❖ *Spinage Tart (Spinach Tart)*	*159*
❖ *Fruit Tarts*	*159*

Index — 160
Notes — 165
Endnotes — 167

a Woman Buying Eggs

Acknowledgments

13

Epicurus brags:"Happiness is a full belly,
The stomach shall be my deity
According to the gullet's dictates.
His temple? – naturally the kitchen –
The source of divine odours."
A most convenient deity,
Who never demands fasting.
Drink before breakfast,
He makes room for it by vomiting.
His table and his wine-bowl
Are true beatitudes.
He always has a skinful,
A bellyful and a flagonful.
Lunch links up with dinner.
His fat cheeks glow red
And his most important blood-vessel (when inflated)
Is stronger than an iron cable.
But the practice of the cult
Provokes acute dyspepsia,
The belly creases up in agony
When you mix your drinks.
The good life is easy
But your stomach's hard at work.
The stomach's reply: "I care for nobody
But myself, and make quite sure
That, gently, for this end,
The digestive juices
Act on food and drink,
While I rest in perfect peace."

From the Carmina Burana
Translation by Richard Smiley
(Master Malcolm McPherson)

Not the Enchanted Ground

a Young Man with Water Bottle and Food Wallet

Errata List

Listed here are major changes since the first edition of the book, especially where we've added or validated an attribution. Where we just added new recipes, we do not note it here. This is so you'll know if one of your favorites has changed or if there was a critical success error (as in the Coffin) in the first book.

We have made some changes to spelling for consistency purposes: Potluck to potluck. Spring form to springform. Pie crust to piecrust. Bread crumbs to breadcrumbs. Aioli, not alioli.

Recipe	Change	Page
Coffin	Amount of water increased	40
Sage Sauce	Amount of Sage changed from *teaspoons to Tablespoons*	45
Braun Pye	*Cloves* added to instructions (had only been in ingredient list in Edition 1)	54
Great Pye	*Rosemary* is called for in the original instructions, but not referred to in the original or the ingredient list.	57
Mincemeat Tart	Moved to an appendix for recipes we can't quite attribute or for which we have provided an updated recipe translation.	157
Hard Sauce	Moved to an appendix for recipes we can't quite attribute or for which we have provided an updated recipe translation.	158
Spinage Tart	Moved to an appendix for recipes we can't quite attribute or for which we have provided an updated recipe translation.	159

Not the Enchanted Ground   Traveling Dysshes

Bringing the Middle Ages to the Potluck

Many SCA members take their clothing, armor, lighting, feast equipment, banners, and tourney furniture seriously, doing research and spending hours to make sure these items create the appropriate medieval and renaissance atmosphere. They then sit down to eat and totally destroy the image, by serving modern foods.

Usually this glaring problem stems from lack of knowledge, inexperience with medieval food, or fear of spending the entire event slaving over a hot cookstove or firepit. Fear Not! Period foods can be prepared for tourneys, encampments, and potlucks easily and conveniently.

The goal for the first edition of this book was to spread knowledge of period foods more widely. After all, eating is one of those things everyone has to do, and you can liken it to wearing period clothes at an SCA event. So, if you can figure out how to have or make at least one tunic, you can figure out how to make at least one SCA food item — or at least how to shop for something more interesting than bread and cheese!

In the last ten years more and more of the "average" SCA attendees have aspired to cook more period dishes, and this is very exciting.

Not the Enchanted Ground

With respect to the estimable Cariadoc and his lady Elizabeth, this booklet is intended for cookery beginners or for those who do not camp or go to tourneys in a totally period manner. We accept Coleman® stoves, ice chests, and plastic to store our food in. Of course, those items are stored out of sight as we continue to strive to keep the ambiance at events as close to that of a medieval encampment as possible.

What foods are acceptable?

Most of us have been told that foods discovered in the New World are not "period" foods, and that tomatoes, potatoes, and soft drinks are excluded. Some know little more. A good starting point is a list of included and excluded foods. As you can see from the food tables on pages 19, there's an amazing variety of food you can eat simply prepared and still be "in period." (This is not an exhaustive list, by any stretch.) We know that some varieties of these foods were grown only in the New World – since we are looking for foods and items which are available commonly in most grocery stores or herb and spice stores, we have not made that distinction in most cases.

Foods in the "Acceptable" category in this listing are clearly Old World, or New World foods that had been accepted as common human food in the Old World by 1600. "No-No's" are foods which are controversial, were not eaten by humans, or which were not widely eaten in the Old World. You may well find

Bringing the Middle Ages to the Potluck   17

recipes, for example, calling for tomatoes or potatoes late in our period (pre-1600). But these foods were not in common use among the wider range of our participants' period of study, and so we have excluded them.

Some of the foods in the list below came to Western Europe from the Middle East and were imported via the land trade routes. If you decide to research what your persona would have eaten, you may want to look into trading habits and be careful about Middle Eastern foods early in our period.

There are few Middle Eastern foods in the recipe section of the booklet, for one good reason: We don't know enough about them to feel that we can give you good information. We have included some of the beverages from the Middle East in the lists of foods, to give those of us who don't want to drink only wine, bear, or mead some other choices. What recipes there are come from Anahita, Duke Cariadoc, or Mistress Elizabeth, whom I consider unimpeachable sources.

Vegetarians

There are few truly vegan recipes in the medieval and renaissance literature, as frugal cooks flavored most dishes, including vegetables, with broths and fats left over from cooking meats and other dishes. However, using either homemade or commercially available vegetarian broths will let you convert many of the cooked vegetable dishes into truly vegan ones. In addition, you can look for Lenten recipes in most period cookbooks and find other vegan recipes.

Ovo-lacto vegetarians will find a sufficiency of foods in the repertoire.

a Beehive

Food Tables

The food tables below are not exhaustive, although we have tried very hard to make them as complete as possible. Please write to the authors with comments, additions, and corrections.

Type of Food	Acceptable	No-No's
Grains	Oats, barley, wheat, rye, rice, millet	Corn (maize), wild rice
Meats and Poultry	Beef, veal, lamb, mutton, pork, venison, rabbit, game hens, quail, chicken, dove, pheasant, goose, duck, swan, guinea hen, pigeon	Turkey
Fish	Most cold-water fish, including: Herring, cod, pollack, stokkfisk, whitefish, mullet, salmon, haddock, trout, bass, perch, eels. Most shellfish, including: mussels, oysters, clam, crab, crayfish, lobster.	Shark, mahi-mahi
Vegetables	Onion, garlic, turnip (greens and root), carrot, cabbage, Brussels sprouts, parsnip (leaves and root), rutabaga (aka swede), red yam, radish, scallion, mustard, beet top (but no root), spinach, artichoke, eggplant, cauliflower, cucumber, nettle (leaf and root), dandelion green, plum tomato (late, Italy and Spain), leaf lettuce, olive, mushroom, borage, summer squash such as: crookneck, zucchini, straightneck, cymling, pattypan, scalloped, Chayotte, butternut (late 1400's, Italian and Islamic), white-flowered gourd (*Lagenaria sicereia*), leek, sea kale (laver)	Potato (began to be introduced in the late 1570's in Spain, grown in England by 1596), capsicum (bell pepper, paprika, chili pepper, etc.), round tomato, okra, pumpkin, lettuce (iceberg, Boston, romaine), broccoli, beet root, yellow sweet potato, winter squash such as: turban, banana, acorn, buttercup, Hubbard, other "variety" squash
Beans and Legumes	Broad (fava) bean, lentil, green (English) pea (very late in period), soybean, haricot bean, chickpea, white (northern) bean, green bean, yellow split pea, green split pea	Lima bean, kidney bean, field pea, black-eyed pea, snow pea, Chinese peapod
Fruits	Bilberry, wild blackberry, damson plum, prune, red raspberry, quince,	Blueberry, cranberry, mango, papaya,

Vegetarians   Traveling Dysshes

	rhubarb, pomegranate, gooseberry, pear, mulberry, black and gold currants, strawberry, apricot, apple, fig, peach, cherry, grape, date, orange, lemon, raisin, honeydew melon, muskmelon (cantaloupe), watermelon, nectarine. Bananas were known very late in our period but not cultivated in the west.	persimmon, cultivated blackberry, avocado, pineapple (although it was being grown in India in the mid-1500's), kiwi, black raspberry, breadfruit.
Nuts	Filbert (hazelnut), chestnut, almond, walnut, acorn, sesame, pistachio, pine nuts	Peanut, pecan, coconut (although they were imported into Persia in the 9th century), cashew, Brazil nut, macadamia nut
Spices and Flavorings	Cinnamon, mace, pepper (black and white), marjoram, cane sugar, oregano, basil, honey, clove, ginger, cubeb, winter and summer savory, dill, cardamom, parsley, sage, rosemary, thyme, wine vinegar, cumin, sandalwood (saunders), saffron, caraway, fennel, tansy, poppy seed, galingale, marigold flowers, rose petals, lavender, hyssop, purslane, nutmeg, rosewater, elderberry, orangewater, sloe, bay leaf, verjuice, lovage	Allspice, capsicum (such as crushed red pepper, paprika, etc.), vanilla, baking powder or baking soda
Dairy Products	Eggs, most hard and soft cheeses (see exceptions in the next column), milk, buttermilk (sometimes used as a leavening, but, alas, most often a pig food!) butter	Yogurt (unless you are Middle Eastern), sour cream, processed cheese. Monterey Jack and Pepper Jack are excluded, as Monterey Jack was invented in California in modern times, and Pepper Jack has modern spices. Colby is also a modern cheese. Bright yellow cheese (most

Food Tables   21

		cheddars2[3]) is acceptable, even though the yellow coloring is a modern (post-1650) phenomenon. "Cream Cheese" is a modern invention4., as is Stilton (a blue-veined cream cheese, invented in the early 1700's)5
Beverages	Wine, mead, small or thin beer, ale, ginger beer, sekanjabin, lemonade, fruit ades, milk (Viking and Mongol), hot coffee (Spain, Moorish, Middle Eastern), fruit sorbet, water, some herb teas (chamomile, yarrow, tansy, willow bark, but mostly for medicinal uses)	Cola, carbonated beverages, root beer (if made from sarsaparilla), Tang, Kool-Aid, coffee, iced or hot black or green tea (Dutch, late 1580's) [Note: we have no evidence that most Western Europeans drank anything but wine, beer/ale, and mead with meals, even though other beverages existed.]

Vegetarians   Traveling Dysshes

What to Serve

Now that we have a wide choice of foods, how should we prepare them? (We've included recipes for some of the foods below which we have ourselves redacted or for which we have permission to reproduce in the recipe section. Others are in the sources listed in the bibliography: for copyright reasons, we do not reproduce them here.)

No Cook Choices

The panicky newcomer or non-cook can safely choose from the following list to make a contribution to any table, be it an encampment at an event or a potluck. For the most part, you can purchase these foods, arrange them nicely on a serving plate, and collect kudos. Even the slimmest pocketbook should be able to find something in the list below that fits the budget.

- Bread (round or football-shaped loaves are more appropriately shaped, and wholegrain or sourdough are more likely to resemble what was served. Breads labeled "European Crusty Bread" or "Peasant Boule" are right on target.)
- Cheese (Cheddar, Edam, Gouda, blue, Brie, goat cheese, mozzarella, Swiss, etc. No Cheez-Whiz® or Velveeta®). Baked Brie is a very nice choice.
- Cooked sausage (such as salami, summer sausage, liverwurst, etc. Sausages with larger "chunks" in their textures more closely resemble those from our period.)
- Cold sliced meat (such as roast beef, pastrami, chicken, etc.)
- Ham (Salt rather than sweet cured preferred)
- Smoked fish
- Roasted or baked chickenfrom the local deli or grocery store (no Kentucky Fried™, please!)
- Precooked pasties or meat pies from local deli or grocery store (Some may have potatoes, but it's a good try.)
- Precooked quiches
- Dolmades (Stuffed grape leaves)
- Tabouli (Middle Eastern)
- Pickled or herbed mushrooms
- Pickle, olives, "pickled garden salad" or "gardiniera" (remove the peppers)
- Pâté (except vegetarian pâté)
- Fruit or nuts
- Applesauce with ginger or mace stirred in
- Fruitcake

What to Serve

- Poppyseed cake
- Shortbread
- Fruit tart (no top crust)
- Dole™ Fruit Ice (and other nondairy ices and sherbets)
- Anything in the Beverage chart that you can buy

Minimal Cook Foods

Most of us can cook something. If you can handle a few basic cooking skills, this list is for you. Many of these dishes can be made in advance and warmed up on site: some require some minimal cooking on site, or transport (say to a potluck) in a warming dish, crock pot, etc.

One of the easiest ways to create a period dish with minimal effort is to roast beef, pork, or chicken, and then serve it with a sauce such as *camaline, galantyne, sage sauce, garlic sauce, jance,* or *pevorade*. Recipes for these sauces are included in the section on Sauces, beginning on page 37. This recipe list has the medieval name for the dish first, and the modern name second. Recipes not included here are found in easily available sources.

- Soppes Dorre (Onions on Toast)
- Roo Broth (Venison Soup)
- Caboges in Potage (Cabbage and Leek Stew)
- Funges (Mushrooms in Broth)
- Ryes of Flessh (Rice in Meat Broth)
- Yrchouns (Sausage Hedgehogs)
- Charlet (Hash with Eggs)
- Sawge Y-farced (Sausage with Sage-Flavored Eggs)
- Herbolet (Herb Custard, or an Omelet)
- Peascoddes (Peas in the Pod)
- Minces (Brussels Sprouts)
- Benes yFride (Fried Beans)
- Salat (Green Salad)
- Peasen Royalle (Green Peas in their own sauce)
- Macrows (Noodles and Cheese)
- Lozenges (Layered Noodles with Cheese)
- Salmon Roste in Sawge (Grilled Salmon Steaks in Sauce)
- Chicke Endored (Gilded Chicken)
- Blackened Chiken (Honey-baked Chicken)
- Garlic Chicken
- Rost Bef with Sawge Aliper (Roast Beef with Garlic-Pepper Sauce)
- Mete y-Forced (Sausage)
- Steykys of Venison or Bef (Beef or Venison Steaks)

Minimal Cook Foods   Traveling Dysshes

- Bourbelier (Roast Pork in Boar Sauce)
- Bardys Bef (Roast Tongue)
- Lorengue de Pouchins (Chicken with Orange Sauce)
- Hotchpodge (Poultry Stew)
- Drye Stewe (Pot Roast)
- Braun en Peraude (Roast Pork with Pepper Sauce)
- Pygge in a Coffin (Ham in Pastry)
- Hericot de Mouton) Lamb or Mutton Stew
- Lange Mortes de Pesoun (Pea Soup with Onions)
- Beef y-Stewed (Braised Beef)
- Peppered Egges (Peppered Eggs)
- Wardonys in Syrypp (Pears in Syrup)
- Pain Perdu (Lost Bread, much like French Toast)
- Frytours of Appels (Apple Fritters)
- Shrewsberry Cakes (Cookies)
- Jumbles (Cookies)
- Appel Moyle (Applesauce)
- Tarte of Applyes (Open-face Apple Pie)
- Daryoles (Custard Tart)

a Threshing Floor

Adventures in Medieval Cooking

If you want to plunge right into medieval cooking, find any of the cookbooks in the sources section and explore. Once you master the recipes that others have translated ("redacted") from medieval and Renaissance sources, you can try your hand at redacting them yourself!

Coping with Camping Technology

Frequently the hardest part of creating a medieval environment at a weekend camping tournament is the cooking. There are ways to make this less onerous: one is to cook ahead, in the comfort of your own kitchen.

Think about this: If you're going to spend all Wednesday or Thursday night making something to take with you, it's just as easy to make a period soup or stew as it is to make spaghetti.

Stews & Soups

Make them no later than Tuesday, freeze them until Friday in Ziploc™6 bags or freezer containers with big mouths (NOT jars unless you're just refrigerating them, or else you'll have to wait until they are completely thawed to get the food out). Use the frozen lumps in your coolers to help chill the other food; it should be defrosted enough to put in a pot and cook by Saturday mid-afternoon.

To finish the soups and stews that have thickeners and special last-minute seasonings: cook the main soup or stew, get the other stuff ready to do at the site. (Buy or grind your bread crumbs early, make the verjuice in advance, measure out the spices in a small sealed jar, etc.) When the stew is hot and bubbly, pretend you've just gotten to that point in the recipe and proceed.

Meats & Sauces

There are a lot of meats and sauces (Beef with Sauce Aliper, Ham with Honey Ginger, etc.) that you can serve on site. Cook the meat in advance, and either freeze or chill and bring in the cooler. Make the sauce on site, cook really HOT (heat, not spicy), slice the meat thin, and serve the sauce over the meat.

Cold Pies

Any cold pie in a coffin (chicken, pigge in a coffin, beef, great pies, etc.) makes an excellent dish to take on a camping trip where you're uncertain if the weather will cooperate (especially if you're cooking over a wood fire). Make in advance (at least by Wednesday), chill well, and bring along for lunch or emergency rations. Pasties and other individual pies work well for this, too, as do cheese tarts, and quiches. (Remember that these take a while to thaw: don't expect to eat it Friday night if you take it out of the deep freeze Friday morning).

Salads & Vegetables

Depending on your trash situation, amount of help available, and patience for prep work, you can either make these ahead or prepare them on site. If you decide to make a green salad or arranged salad on site, bring the ingredients, chilled, and put to work those folk who claim they are only good for peeling vegetables. If you want to do much of the prep work at home, peel, chill, and bring in plastic of one sort or another in a cooler.

If you are short on ice, be sure to put meat leftovers in the ice, and toss the leftover veggies. Of course, one hopes never to have too *many* leftovers.

Refrigeration, Food Management, & Relaxation

Siobhan managed at Pennsic Wars for 15 years to feed up to 40 people for two weeks on a daily basis with at least dinner (and sometimes lunch and dinner) from period sources. (Breakfast and fighters being what they are, breakfasts are everyone's favorite comfort food.) Cooking is one of her major forms of medieval recreation, so for her it's pleasure rather than a chore. We know it's not to everyone's taste, so we've tried to include easier dishes as well as more challenging ones.

The first 3 to 5 days she cooks out of coolers and the local fruit and veggie stand; and the secret to this is using a deep freeze to freeze things while you are still at home, managing access to the coolers religiously, and using dry ice if you can get it. Be sure your coolers are of high quality. The Styrofoam® boxes sold at some grocery stores and drug stores are not adequate. (Check *Consumer Reports* for their recommendations; we use Coleman, Rubbermaid, and Gott brands).

(Please note: Cariadoc and Elizabeth teach a really great class in how to preserve foods to eliminate the need for refridgeration at all while you're camping. It's well worth checking out if you get the chance.)

The rest of the time (up to 12 days) we cook with a trip to the grocery store every other day for fresh meat and such. So most of those techniques are well tested and intended to let you feel more like you're camping in a medieval encampment without feeling like a kitchen drudge to boot. We aim to spend no more than 2 hours getting dinner on the table for the masses, and lunch shouldn't take more than ½ hour.

What to Serve

It's critical to keep the cold foods cold. We don't want to introduce food poisoning to our audiences as well as new food experiences. If you can't manage the coolers and ice to handle this, don't attempt to store food for several days at a time.

a Young Couple Pressing Grapes at the Harvest

Emergency Rations

Specifically at SCA camping trips and outdoor events, some emergency rations are a smart move. What do you do if a thunderstorm and drenching rain drops the temperature 25 degrees and folks who were complaining of the heat (and possibly having problems with heat stress) are cold, wet, and have the beginnings of hypothermia? We carry dried soups as emergency rations for camping trips. While in the Western part of the country you more often worry about blistering heat spells than cold snaps, having something available with salt and warmth that can be fixed quickly is a smart move. (Even if you plan to cook over an open firepit the entire time, taking at least a small stove and fuel is a smart move. It can stay in the supply tent if unneeded.)

Gatorade and other sports drinks that replace electrolytes are also good to carry, particularly in the dried form where they can be stashed in your camping box and left until needed. Even if they have gotten hot and fossilized into hard lumps they can be turned into useful drinks for folks who are heat stressed or hypothermic. Half-strength Gatorade is the best way to replenish both fluids and electrolytes. If you are short on Gatorade but have fruit drinks such as lemonade or orange juice, mix 1 tsp table salt with 2 quarts juice, and add an extra can of water to the mix. If you are in dire straits with no medical help around, make up your dried soups and feed them to the stressed person. The salt and broth are restorative.

Candy bars (chocolate or chocolate with nuts), dried meat or cheese, and crackers or bread (essentially, things which do not require cooking but which provide protein and energy) are also good to stock.

Bees and Skeps

Where to find it

With the popularity of ethnic cooking in the United States, most of us can find nearly all the spices and herbs we want right on the supermarket shelves. But not everything is at the local hypermarket, and not every town has a large ethnic community to encourage merchants to carry more esoteric items.

This section includes hints on where to find herbs, spices, and other items such as smoked fish, venison, and so on. We have included establishments that can be found at large SCA events such as Pennsic and Estrella, in most large cities, shop-by-mail stores, and, the most recent addition to the global marketplace, shopping on the Internet.

You should also stop by your local library and check out the cooking magazines, such as *Gourmet*, to look at the ads for food suppliers. *New Yorker*, *Yankee*, and other up-scale magazines also have good ads.

Large SCA Events

At Pennsic and Estrella you can usually find the Pepperer's Guild, and other SCA merchants who carry an assortment of medieval herbs and spices such as cubebs, summer savory, saunders (sandalwood), indigo, woad, and so on. They also have shop-by-mail addresses for the rest of the year.

❖ **Astrid's Herbals**
   Trinette L. Kern
   1037 Francis Road
   Pittsburgh, PA 15234

❖ **Freya's Garden**
   Genvieve. Malm-Sather
   1037 Francis Road
   Pittsburgh, PA 15234

❖ **Herbals & Oddities**
   Ruth Cardiff
   13066 Marsh Rd.
   Bealeton, VA 22712

❖ **Lion's Nest Trading Post**
   Charlotte Hoover
   RR 18 Box 66
   Bedford, IN 47421

❖ **Pepperer's Guild, The**
Jeffery D. Russell
Box 174
Glastonbury, CT 08025

❖ **Sands of Thyme**
Troy Shearer
123 Centennial Ave.
Hanover, PA 17331

❖ **Sign of the Black Rose**
Christina Baum
2447 North 4th St.
Columbus, OH 43202-2706

Local Non-Supermarket Sources

Looking in your own neighborhood for fresh spices, herbs, dairy products, and vegetables? ? Try:
- Natural foods stores and restaurants
- Vegetarian restaurants
- Natural dyers

Natural food co-ops

Food cooperatives are member-owned natural foods stores providing high quality foods, goods and services to consumers. Many co-ops carry a variety of organically grown, minimally processed and packaged, often in bulk; grains, beans, nuts, baked goods, produce, refreshments, herbs and spices, dairy products and frozen foods, as well as environmentally safe household products and health and beauty aids.

If you want to find good sources of non-standard meat (rabbit, venison, etc.) and poultry (pheasant, quail, etc.), try:
- 4-H auctions (lambs, mutton, veal, beef, chicken)
- Wholesale butchers (ask at a restaurant whose meat you like)
- Specialty poulterers (Look the phone book: sometimes they are listed under "game farms")
- Local co-op farms
- Agricultural colleges – the poultry club, lamb club, and other animal husbandry groups frequently sell high quality meat and eggs at quite reasonable prices as a fundraiser.

Shop-by-Mail

Most of the establishments listed below have catalogues that you can request. Be sure and check for the current prices before ordering.

❖ **Chiltern Seeds**
Bortree Stile
Ulverston, Cumbria LA12 7PB
ENGLAND

❖ **Colonial Garden Kitchens**
POB 66
Hanover, PA 17333-0066
(800) 258-6702

❖ **Country Cheese**
2101 San Pablo Ave.
Berkeley, CA
(510) 841-0752

❖ **Fine Gardening Magazine**
The Taunton Press
63 South Main St.
POB 5506
Netson, CT 06470-5506

❖ **Flatbush Food Coop Herbs and Spices**
1318 Cortelyou Road
Brooklyn, NY 11226
(718) 284-9717
coop@dorsai.org
http://www.dorsai.org/~coop/

❖ **The Gourmet Gardener**
8650 College Blvd., Suite 205IN
Overland Park, KS 66210-1806
(913) 345-0490
fax (913) 451-2443
http://metroux.metrobbs.com/tgg/herbs.htm

❖ Gustav Paulig Ltd
Iiluodonkuja 2
POB 15
00981 Helsinki
FINLAND
Int + 358-0-31-981
http://www.mofile.fi/biz/paulig/

❖ The Herb Companion
Interweave Press
201 East Fourth Street
Loveland, CO 80537-5655
(800) 456-5835
Fax (970) 669-6117
HerbCompanion@Interweave.com
 www.discoverherbs.com

❖ In Good Taste
13502 Whittier Blvd., Suite H-190
Whittier, CA 90605
(310) 465-4611

❖ Lhasa Karnak
2513 Telegraph Ave.
Berkeley, CA
(510) 548-0380

❖ Nadine's Smokehouse
POB 1787
65 Fowler Ave
Torrington, CT 06790
(800) 222-2059

❖ Nichol's Garden Nursery
1198 Pacific West
Albany, OR 97321
(503) 928-9280

❖ Penzeys, Ltd. Spice House
POB 1448
Waukesha, WI 52187
(414) 574-0277 (hours: Monday through Saturday 9 - 5)

Where to find it

- **Ratto's Deli & Restaurant**
  821 Washington St
  Oakland, CA
  (510) 832-6503

- **Sandy Bay Saffron Company**
  Palo Alto, CA
  Sandybay@ix.netcom.com

- **The Souk**
  Pike Place Market
  1969 Pike Place
  Seattle, WA 98101
  (206) 441-1666

- **The Spice House**
  1102 North 3rd St.
  Milwaukee, WI 53203

- **Spice Merchant**
  POB 524
  Jackson Hole, WY 83001
  (307) 733-7811
  http://eMall.Com/Spice/Spice1.html

- **Tenzing Momo and Co.**
  93 Pike
  Seattle, WA 98101
  (206) 623-9837

3 Women Dining Outdoors

Making Do

*(Or what to use if you don't have
a partridge in your pear tree)*

Sometimes a sauce sounds good, or a baking recipe, but you just don't have doves or quail on hand to try it out. What do you do? Some of the recipes have substitutes listed right in the recipe. (No cook has everything on hand all the time!)

A good general introduction to spices can be found at Gernot Katzer's Spice Pages [http://www-ang.kfunigraz.ac.at/~katzer/engl/generic_frame.html]

These tables include more period substitutes for period ingredients, to help you resist the temptation to include more modern ingredients.

The Recipe Calls for (Meats)	Substitute
Blood	Same volume of red wine or water mixed with 1 tsp flour per cup of blood called for, and ½ tsp Marmite or other gravy darkener. (This will NOT work in blood pudding or sausage.)
Boar	Pork roast (ask the butcher for a large one)
Dolphin	Tuna
Goose	Duck (use less oil in the marinade)
Guinea hen	Goose, Cornish game hen, chicken
Pheasant, swan	Goose (but not duck)
Quail eggs	Small hen's eggs
Rabbit	Fryer chicken, hen pieces
Veal	Very tender beef (pound if necessary)
Venison	Pork loin, center-cut pork chops, pork roast, beef flank, coarse ground round or chuck, chuck roast, top round steak (venison is very lean compared to all these meats; trim all excess fat)
Whole quail, dove	Small Cornish game hens
Whole rabbit	Whole chicken (and pray your guests are city-bred)

Making Do 35

The Recipe Calls for (Fruits, vegetables, spices)	Substitute
Black grapes	Red grapes
Chives	Scallion tops, cut very fine
Cubeb	Cubebs are pungent and bitter, and some describe their aroma as reminding one of turpentine. In general, cubebs are variously described as dry-woody, warm-camphoraceous and spicey-peppery. The general rule has been to substitute black pepper, but if you want to get the real bitter flavor you can try ½ freshly ground black pepper and ½ ground fresh ground ginger, or ½ ground black pepper and ½ ground allspice
Juice of one lemon	3 Tbsp lemon juice
Lovage	Celery leaves
Parsnips	Turnips
Pears	Canned pears, apples (If the pears are to be mashed up, add 5 peeled seedless grapes per apple.)
Rutabagas (swedes)	½ parsnips and ½ carrots
Saffron	2 drops yellow food coloring, 1 drop red (for very small batches, use tiny quantities on the tip of a toothpick) [Note: this simulates the color, but does nothing to simulate the flavor.]
Saunders	Red food coloring (similar note about flavor as saffron)
Summer savory	Winter savory
Tart or crab apples	Apples plus 1 tsp lemon juice per apple
Vinegar	Lemon juice, or ½ tsp meat tenderizer and same volume of water
Wine	Water in same volume [warning, this will change the flavor], vinegar, lemon juice, grape juice (Use these acidic juices especially in meats, where the wine will tenderize the meat; add good coloring if the wine was supposed to lend color.)
Wine vinegar	Cider or white vinegar. NOT Balsamic vinegar

Shop-by-Mail   Traveling Dysshes

Recipes

The following recipes have been translated (redacted) from the original medieval and renaissance sources. With each recipe the person who redacted the recipe, the original source, time period, and place of origin is noted.

We do not have a glossary of cooking terms in this booklet, for space reasons. A really good place to find cooking terms defined is at A Boke of Gode Cookery, an online website at:
http://www.godecookery.com/glossary/glossary.htm

Measurement Unit	Abbreviation
teaspoon	Tsp.
Tablespoon	Tbsp.
ounce	Oz
pound	Lb.
Fahrenheit	F.

Many of these recipes use common spices and ingredients available at either a full-service grocery store, a health food store, an oriental or ethnic food market. Because this booklet is designed for beginners, recipes calling for more exotic spices are left for later discovery.

In most instances spice measurements are for dried spices, as they are the most commonly available. If you have fresh spices available, season cautiously unless you're very familiar with the relative proportions of fresh spices to dried spices. For example, ¼ cup of fresh basil equals 1/8 tsp dried basil.

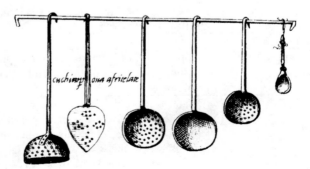

a Rack of Implements

Common Items

There are some items, like "cinnamon sugar" or "barbeque sauce" in our kitchens, which are generally known to most cooks but every cook has her or his own variety of it. Perhaps your family makes "Cinnamon sugar" with mace and nutmeg. Or, like Siobhan, perhaps you put beer in your barbeque sauce.

The same was true in medieval times. You will find recipes calling for *powder forte* (strong powder) – and we can assure you they don't mean gunpowder or some thing else! We've listed some of these items below, along with instructions on how to make some common items that our sources assume "everyone" knows how to make.

❖ Powder Douce

Powder douce is 'sweet powder' or "blanche poudre," and was another "generic" spice mixture on the shelves of medieval and renaissance cooks, only this time composed of sweet spices instead of savory.

At base, you need 2 parts cinnamon to 1 part sugar (sugar being considered a spice in period). Other components can be ginger, galingale, nutmeg, mace, bay leaf, and in some areas you might find fennel (still used in some parts of the world as a "breath sweetener"), cloves, anise, cubebs and grains of paradise, depending on taste and spice cupboard contents. You may make up your mixture based on the audience you expect for the food, as well, as some folks new to medieval cooking may need to be eased into the concept that anise or cloves are a "sweet" spice (you can remind them about licorice or pumpkin pie).

Powder douce can also contain saffron, but many folks seem to have aversion to saffron, so it may not be a good general call. A good starter recipe is:

Ingredients:

1 Tbsp ginger
1 Tbsp fine white sugar (some folks use powdered sugar)
2 Tbsp mace
3 Tbsp cinnamon

Directions:

In a clean mortar, put all the spices together and mix well with a spoon. Use the pestle to finely grind them together. (Some folks put the whole mix in a small blender jar and run it at high speed. You need a larger quantity of powder for this to work well, however.) Store in a labeled, tightly capped jar or bottle. Be sure to note the date you made the mixture, as after six months or so it may need to be replaced or "enlivened." (Some folk keep their spice mixes going as one would a sourdough starter, adding in new spices every few months.)

❖ Powder Forte

Powder forte or "strong powder" was a common spice mix, routinely used by cooks in medieval and renaissance cuisine for seasoning food. It is rather like today's curry powder or five-spice powder, which are blends of several different herbs and spices, but which vary by manufacturer and even by region where sold.

The components of powder forte varied from cook to cook, but were basically strong spices such as black pepper, long pepper, cubeb, cloves, nutmeg, mace, cinnamon, ginger, etc. There could be as few as two or three ingredients or as many as a half dozen or more. All ingredients should be freshly ground. Siobhan's recipe is:

Ingredients:

½ tsp fresh ginger
½ tsp fresh nutmeg
½ tsp mace powder
1 tsp finely ground black pepper
½ tsp grains of paradise, ground
½ tsp cubeb, ground

Directions:

In a mortar, put all the spices together and mix well with a spoon. Use the pestle to finely grind them together. (Some folks put the whole mix in a small blender jar and run it at high speed. You need a larger quantity of powder for this to be really effective, however.) Store in a labeled, tightly capped jar or bottle. Be sure to note the date you made the mixture, as after six months or so it may need to be replaced or "enlivened." (Some folk keep their spice mixes going as one would a sourdough starter, adding in new spices every few months.)

a Ring-necked Pheasant

❖ Almond Milk

Almond milk is a flavoring that is also the primary liquid in many recipes. It's easy to make, and can make a substantial difference in how the recipe comes out. As you can guess, in period real milk from whatever animal did not store well at room temperature, and not all people had cold rooms or butteries. Medieval cooks turned to the liquid that results when you grind almonds or walnuts. The resulting liquid, high in natural fats, could be prepared fresh whenever needed, the quantity available was limited only by how many nuts were on hand. It also could be made well ahead of time and stored with no danger of degeneration. Because of its high fat content, it could be churned into butter just like animal milk. However, because it did *not* come from animals, it could be used during Church designated meatless days.

Almost every SCA cook has his or her own recipe, but here's how Siobhan makes it. There is also a good description in Scully's *The Art of Cookery in the Middle Ages,* 1995.

Ingredients:

1 ½ cups raw almonds, shelled
2 cup boiling water

Directions:

Finely grind your almonds (a food processor or blender is best for this, but you can grate them on a cheese grater). Pour the boiling water over them, and steep for 5-8 minutes, or until the liquid is white and very cloudy. Sieve the mixture (cheesecloth over a medium-sized sieve or colander is good), removing all the large grains. Store the resulting liquid in a tightly capped jar until used.

Some people use their food processor or blender to puree the almonds and liquid together, more or less homogenizing it and improving the fat content and protein. We can see the reasoning behind this, but some folks prefer not to do this since our medieval forebears couldn't have done it, and instead assume that a nut "meal" of the approximate fineness as cornmeal would result from grinding in a mortar or pestle or a grindstone. Personally, Siobhan uses the "dregs," if any, in modern treats such as brownies or in other period items where the faint remaining flavor of almonds would be good, such as strawberry pudding or seedcake.

❖ Breadcrumbs

Breadcrumbs are a basic thickener for sauces, stews, and other period dishes. In general, if the recipe says to "thicken" something, breadcrumbs are a good bet as the mechanism. There is a substantial difference between commercial breadcrumbs and the ones you make at home. Basically, if you want to use commercial breadcrumbs you must start with one-third of the amount called for in the recipe and add more cautiously. Commercial breadcrumbs are substantially drier than those made in your home kitchen, and absorb lots more liquid.

Making your own breadcrumbs can be a lot of fun, and it's a great way to use up stale or unused bread after a feast or camping trip. Your success will depend on what you start with: drier breads yield, not surprisingly, drier, more easily ground breadcrumbs.

If you use commercial white sandwich bread, drying the bread takes longer than it does with homemade bread or breads such as Italian, French, or Sourdough loaves.

Ingredients:

6 slices of standard sandwich bread

Directions:

Heat oven to 300° F. Put a cooling rack on top of a cookie sheet, and place the bread on the rack, well separated. Turn the oven down to 250, and put the bread on a middle rack. Set a timer for 30 minutes and go embroider something.

At 30 minutes, test a piece of the bread. If it still bends, put it back in the oven for another 15-20 minutes. When the bread shatters and crumbles rather than bends and breaks, it's done.

Remove from the oven. Some folks cut the crusts off at this stage, but they are generally as easy to turn into crumbs as anything else. Put one or two slices in a reclosable storage bag (1 gallon is a good size) and, on a solid surface such as a counter top, marble slab, or butcher-block, roll the bread bag with a rolling pin. Turn the bag over and around until the bread is reduced to fine crumble. Pour out of the plastic bag into a storage container and repeat for the rest of the bread. Makes about 1 cup of crumbs.

Store in a tightly capped container, preferably in the freezer. Leaving the crumbs exposed to the air can help you recreate the invention of penicillin.

Common Items   41

❖ Paste (Flaky Pie Crust)

This is a short crust, something to be enjoyed with sweet pies, rather than the coffin, which is more like architectural material. There are a lot of recipes, but in general they are all like this one, which Cordelia's mom taught her!

Ingredients:

1 ½ cups bleached all purpose flour
½ tsp salt
1/3 cup vegetable shortening
3 Tbsp cold water (approximate)
¼ tsp ground cinnamon (optional)
4 Tblsp sugar (optional)

To make a top and bottom, change ingredients to:
2 cups flour
½ tsp salt
½ cup ice water
½ tsp cinnamon
6 Tblsp sugar

Directions:

Sift dry ingredients into large bowl. Work shortening in with pastry cutter or 2 forks until lumps are pea size. Sprinkle the cold water over the mixture and blend until mixture clings to itself. Form a flattened ball. Place ball back into the bowl, cover with plastic wrap and refrigerate for at least one hour.

Preheat oven and find your 9" pie plate. Place the ball of dough between 2 sheets of waxed paper and roll with large rolling pin into a circle about 11" across, gently remove one layer of waxed paper and using the other, pick up the circle of dough and gently place it over the pie plate. Remove the waxed paper and press the dough into the pie plate. Make fancy edge and refrigerate again (this reduces shrinkage when the crust is baked.

Preheat oven to 425 degrees F.

If the filling is to baked as well, fill the crust now and bake the pie according to directions.

If the crust is to be cooked before filling, prick the bottom of the crust with a fork and bake 12 to 15 minutes, or until the edge of the crust is nicely browned. Cool on a wire rack to room temperature before filling.

Paste (Flaky Pie Crust)   Traveling Dysshes

❖ A Coffin

In period, most "savory" pies and many sweet ones would use a standing piecrust rather than the short crust we associate with pastries and pies today. A standing piecrust is usually not eaten completely but serves as a cooking and serving vessel for the filling. (Some folks really like eating the crust soaked in gravy. Most people don't like the crust much and just eat the filling.)

Coffins were also highly decoratedd. For example, tiny pigs made out of dough (or pricked into the cover without penetrating it) would indicate a pork pie. Alternately, heraldic images make nice decorations for pies. There are sets of tiny cookie cutters available that make really nice decorative pieces. Recently, Siobhan has been experimenting with interlaced initials for the recipients of the pie, either cut out of dough with a sharp knife or made of rolled "snakes" of dough.

We use the boiled fat and water method. It makes a tough but very sturdy (my lord calls them "studly") coffin that will support itself and the filling up to about 12" high. It is great for sotelties and decoration. Recent reading indicates that not only could we use coffins for enclosing standing pies and meats, but also could make them as serving dishes for soups, etc., after baking them and glazing them with a milk-and-water mixture.

Duchess Caellyn FitzHugh gave this recipe to Siobhan, and implied that it was combined from several sources, including the original *Mrs. Beeton's Guide to Household Management.*

This recipe will fit a 6" springform pan. Double it for a 10" pan.

Ingredients:

4 ½ cups plain flour, sifted (A flour with high-gluten content helps here.)
½ cup butter (1 stick if you buy it that way), or half shortening and half butter
(or ½ cup lard for really STIFF dough, mostly for sotelties, etc.)
1 cup hot water (adjust a little depending on how well the dough comes out – it should be the consistency of PlayDough®) *[Note: This is a correction from the original edition of this booklet. The first edition called for ¼ cup of water, which is clearly not enough.]*
¼ tsp salt

Making the coffin:

Put the flour in a large bowl and mix with salt; make a well in the center. Boil the fat and water; mix quickly into the flour. Let it sit 4–5 minutes, or until it is cool enough to handle. (Siobhan uses her microwave to boil the water and fat — less chance of the fat catching fire on the stove, and a whole lot easier to boot.)

When it forms a ball, knead into elastic consistency and then quickly press it into your form. (I have used springform pans, including one gorgeous oval-

Common Items   43

shaped one from Germany that is 7" high; formed the dough around the outside
of tuna cans for individual coffins; around a cardboard mold for a square castle;
and so on.) This amount of dough makes the base and sides for an 8"
springform and a thin cover; it won't do a whole lot more.

Press 2/3 of the dough into the form using your fingertips, working fairly
fast before the dough cools. Cover the leftover part for the lid with waxed paper
or cling film and a towel to keep it hot while you work. Leave a generous
overhang (1/2") on the sides of the form for connecting the cover.

The dough should be no less than ¼" and no more than 1/3" thick for a
standing pie. Try to avoid the huge bottom problem, but be aware that you do
need a sturdy bottom of the wall to support itself when the springform is
removed.

If you form the dough around the outside of a mold (the way they did it in
period), be sure to remove the form before filling the pie. Duchess Caellyn
FitzHugh taught me to make a heavy-duty tin-foil "collar" around the outside to
take the place of a springform support, then bake as below. Mrs. Beeton's pork
pie is made with waxed paper wrapped and pinned around the outside of the
walls of the coffin for support, and to prevent over browning. Baking parchment
would also work.

Filling the coffin:

Pack the mold with your filling. This pie does NOT expand much, so you
can fill it pretty full. (And, in fact, a densely packed filling helps support the
walls.) Sometimes we add the liquid after the meat filling and cook it with the
filling; other times the hot liquid is added after cooking, and cools and congeals
along with the pie.

For dry-ish fillings, such as beef or pork, c liquid is good, because the pie
can be deadly dry without it. (Obviously your architecture stands or falls here; if
the liquid stays in when you cook it, it worked. For this reason, I prefer to add
liquid to pork or beef after the pie is cooked.)

Decorating the coffin:

Roll out the cover about ½ inch larger than the top of the coffin; attach by
working the extra material for the sides together with the extra edge of the
cover. Roll the dough inward to the center of the pie: if the crust connection
hangs outside the springform edge it may break off when you take the
springform off. You can do cool crenelations, rolls, etc., as this dough has the
consistency of PlayDough™. Save a little bit for cutout decorations.

If the recipe calls for adding the broth *after* the pie is baked, cut a small
(one inch diameter max) hole in the top of the crust. You can decorate around
the hole as you wish. After the pie is finished, pour the hot liquid *slowly* in
through this hole. 7

A Coffin   Traveling Dysshes

Make whatever cool decorations you think would be fun at this time. Attach the decorations to the cover with water or egg.

Preheat the oven to 450 degrees F. Cook the filled coffin for 15 to 20 minutes, take it out, remove the springform, wash the outside with beaten egg and water, put it back in the oven. Reduce the heat to 350; cook for 30 to 50 minutes more. (More or less depends on whether your filling was cooked in advance. Don't bake less than 30 minutes here or the crust will not be cooked through at the base of the "walls". If your filling was uncooked, bake about 50 minutes.)

If when you start to take off the springform the coffin doesn't "feel" right, or if it appears that it is buckling (more than just a little bit of outward bulge), put it back on and bake for another 10 to 15 minutes.

Serve cold for excellent cold pies. (They travel well for wars, picnics, potlucks, feasts, etc.) If you freeze a full-sized standing pie [6 - 8" diameter or more], it takes a good 24 hours to thaw in the fridge or a cooler, so beware!

Other uses

Bartolomeo Scappi (1570's) suggests using coffins as serving dishes for chopped meats, stews, soups, etc. Create the coffin and cover, wash inside and out with the egg and water mixture, bake coffin and cover separately until they are hard and standing alone. Fill with a cooked filling; cover and serve. (Here we're stumped; the reading doesn't tell how to keep the cover on. Presumably one of those "everybody knew" things.) Experience says that soups and such had best be served promptly, although we would expect the coffin to stand up for about 20 minutes before soaking through.

Only one of Robert May's meat pie recipes indicates that the coffin and cover are to be prebaked before filling with precooked ingredients, then baked.

Most of May's fruit and other tarts/pies are to be covered with cut covers. The drawings for the cut covers are quite elaborate, and quite impossible to shape after baking.

❖ Verjuice

Take tart grapes, apples, crab apples, or any other tart or unripe fruit. Work in a food processor or food mill. Strain to obtain the sour juice.

Verjuice is now commercially available in Arabic specialty stores (look for "sour grape juice") and from some vineyards

Sauces   45

Sauces

As mentioned before, the easiest way to convert a modern meat into a period dish is by serving a medieval sauce with it or over it. This is a listing of some of the more interesting and most popular sauces.

Some sauces are much like what we consider gravy; some sauces are condiments, similar to cranberry sauce or mint jelly. All are intended to complement the meat. Unless otherwise noted, serve the sauce on the side, piping hot.

Most of these sauce recipes make about 1 cup of sauce.

❖ Sage Sauce

Siobhan Medhbh, Two Fifteenth-Century Cookery-Books, 1430-1450, England and France

This sauce is excellent for pork or ham. You can serve over hot or cold meat. Some folks like this sauce cold, when it jellies.

Original:

Take the yolks of cooked eggs and sage and grinde hem small; stepe broth and creme and vynegar and styr hem smooth. Cast in the eggs and strayne until smooth. Make it hot and serve it forth.

Ingredients:

4 yolks of hard-boiled eggs
4 Tbsp (aka ¼ cup) fresh sage, chopped fine
2 Tbsp vinegar
½ cup chicken or beef broth
½ cup heavy cream

Directions:

Mash the egg yolks with the chopped sage and 1 Tbsp vinegar to a smooth paste. Put in a small saucepan.

Over low heat, whisk in the broth and cream gradually, making sure it does not curdle. When the sauce is blended smooth, taste.

Add the rest of the vinegar if necessary, whisking constantly. Heat to medium heat (but do not boil). Pour over sliced ham or pork.

Sage Sauce   Traveling Dysshes

❖ Sawse Cameline (Cinnamon Sauce)

Katerine, Le Menagier, 1393, Paris

This recipe appears in a variety of sources; all have cinnamon in them. Recommended for roast veal, rabbit, and lamb, and I rather like it with tender roast pork.

Original:

Note that at Tourney to make cameline they bray ginger, cinnamon and saffron and half a nutmeg moistened with wine, then take it out of the mortar; then have white breadcrumbs, not toasted but moistened in cold water and brayed in the mortar, moisten them with wine and strain them, then boil all together and put in brown sugar last of all; and that is winter cameline. And in summer they do the same, but it is not boiled.

And in truth, to my taste, the winter sort is good, but in [summer] that which followeth is far better; bray a little ginger and a great deal of cinnamon, then take it out and have toasted bread moistened, or plenty of bread raspings in vinegar,, brayed and strained.

Ingredients:

¼ cup raisins
¼ cup nutmeats (walnuts or hazelnuts are good)
½ tsp each ground ginger and ground cinnamon
1/8 tsp ground cloves
2 slices of bread, baked dry and broken into chunks (or an equal amount of the
    hard crusts from crusty bread)
½ tsp salt
1/3 - ½ cup wine vinegar

Directions:

In a food processor or food mill, grind all the ingredients (except the vinegar) at once until everything is finely chopped. (Otherwise, chop the raisins, nuts, and bread finely and stir together with the rest.)

Mix with the vinegar until it reaches a chutney or relish-like consistency. Salt to taste; serve cold with the meat (in a separate dish or alongside the meat as a dipping sauce or relish).

Sauces

❖ Garlek Cameline (Garlic Cinnamon Sauce)

Siobhan Medhbh, Le Menagier, 1393, Paris

Le Menagier recommends this sauce for fried white fish; I also like it with breast of chicken or goose.

Original:

Crush garlic, cassia and bread, and steep in vinegar.

Ingredients:

1 tsp ground ginger
2 cloves garlic, mashed or pressed
1 slice bread, toasted and rolled to fine crumbs
¼ cup vinegar
salt to taste

Directions:

Grind the ginger, garlic, and breadcrumbs together.

Warm the vinegar in a small saucepan and add the rest; stir or whisk until everything blends together and begins to thicken. If it seems too dry, add a little more vinegar or water. Serve hot with the fish or chicken.

Fishing

❖ Cormarye (Caraway Sauce for Pork)

Katerine, Forme of Cury, 1390, England and France

Ideally you will cook the pork roast with this sauce, and thicken and serve the remaining sauce afterward. But if you have leftover pork to spruce up, or have otherwise acquired a pork roast, you can make the sauce separately.

Original:

Take colyaundre, caraway smale grounden, powdour of peper and garlec ygrounde, in red wine; medle alle this togyder and salt it. Take loynes of porkrawe and fle of the skyn, and pryk it wel with a knyf, and lay it in the sawse. Roost it whan thou wilt, & kepe that which fallith therfro in the rostyng and seethe it in a possynet with fair broth, & serue it forth.

Ingredients:

1 tsp each coriander and caraway seeds
3 cloves garlic, crushed
½ cup red wine
½ tsp salt
½ tsp fresh ground pepper
½ cup beef broth
3 Tbsp drippings from the roasted pork – optional

Directions:

Grind the seeds together. A really tough blender will work, or a sturdy food processor. Some folks reserve a small coffee mill for jobs like this. The more finely you can crush the seeds, the better.

Mix the crushed seeds with the garlic, salt, pepper, and wine, preferably in a blender or food processor.

(If you are roasting the pork yourself, start the roast now. Pour this mixture over it and roast 25 minutes per pound at 350 degrees F. Baste the roast every 15 minutes or so with the juices from the pan plus some extra red wine. When the roast is done, pour off the drippings into a saucepan.) If you are refreshing roast pork, put all the previous ingredients in a saucepan. Add the drippings or some oil.

Add beef broth. Stir and bring to a boil. If you want, you can thicken with breadcrumbs and vinegar.. Serve hot on the side.

Sauces   49

❖ Jance Sawse (Walnut Garlic Sauce)

Siobhan Medhbh, Two Fifteenth-Century Cookery-Books, 1430-1450, England and France

Recommended for white fishes (cod, halibut) as well as gamier poultry (goose, duck). This sauce is also referenced in Le Menagier, where it is described as using almonds and verjuice, but the recipe itself is not found in there. This redaction is a combination of the two.

Original:

Take curnylles of walnotyes, and clouys of garlecke, and piper, brede, and salt, and cast al in a morter; and grynde it smal, & tempre it with the same brothe that the fysshe was sode in, and serue it forthe.

Ingredients:

4 Tbsp ground walnuts
3 cloves of garlic, mashed
½ tsp ginger
½ cup verjuice (see page 44)
¼ cup broth

Directions:

Grind the ginger, walnuts, and garlic together. Warm the verjuice to boiling in a small saucepan. Whisk everything together until it has just begun to thicken. Leave on very low heat for the flavors to blend while you cook the fish or finish the poultry. Stir in the broth a few minutes before you serve; warm the sauce again while you stir in the broth (but do not boil).

❖ Piper Sauce (Pepper Sauce)

Cordelia Toser, Pleyn Delit first ed., Ashmole 1439

This sauce is a good accompaniment for roast venison, goose, or veal. It also refreshes a cold roast beef marvelously.

Original:

Take brede, and frye it in grece, draw it vp with brothe and vinegre; caste ther-to poudre piper, and salt, sette on the fire, boile it, and messe it forth.

Ingredients:

3 slices bread
1 Tbsp butter
2 cups beef broth
1 Tbsp wine vinegar
1 tsp salt
½ tsp black pepper

Directions:

Fry bread in butter until it starts to brown. Remove from heat, and pour a little hot broth over the bread and soak until softened. Puree all ingredients in blender or food processor.

Return puree to saucepan and cook over medium heat until thickened

a Man Eating His Wife's Cooking

❖ Sawse Gauncile (Garlic Sauce)

Siobhan Medhbh, Two Fifteenth-Century Cookery-Books, 1430-1450, England and France

If you make this sauce without saffron, it is "garleck sawse" for poultry; if you add the saffron it becomes "sawse gauncile" for boiled or roasted pork.

"Sawse Gauncile" is one of the few examples of a sauce made with flour and milk in the cooking literature of the period. It's familiar to us because we use a lot of white sauces, but it's an unusual recipe for the period.

Original:

Take milke and a litul floure, And cast hit in a potte, And lette boile al togidur al thyn; and whan hit is wel boyled, take and stampe garleck small, and caste there-to pouder of peper, and salt, And then serue it forthe.

Ingredients:

1 ½ cup milk
2 Tbsp flour
2 Tbsp butter
3 cloves garlic, minced fine
pinch salt
pinch saffron (optional)

Directions:

Melt the butter; make a paste of the flour and butter. Add the milk slowly over medium heat, whisking constantly as the mixture thickens. (This is essentially a white sauce, and is one of the few documented places where we see a "roux" as is seen later in modern cookbooks.)

Mix in the garlic. Salt to taste. Simmer for 5-10 minutes, and serve spooned over sliced meat.

GARLIC

❖ Verde Sawse (Green Sauce)

Katerine, Forme of Cury, 1390, England
Best with fish: poached, grilled, or sautéed.

Original:

Take persel, mynt, garlek, a litul serpell and sauge; a litul canel, gynger, piper, wyne, brede, vyneger; do thereto powdour of gynger and peper, & the grece of the maulard. Salt it; boile it wel and serue it forth.

Ingredients:

2 Tbsp fresh parsley, finely minced
2 Tbsp fresh garlic, chopped
1 Tbsp each dried mint, rosemary, sage (you may also use any combination of thyme, sorrel, savory, and the above) or 2 Tbsp each finely minced fresh herbs
2-4 Tbsp finely crushed dry breadcrumbs
¼ - ½ tsp salt to taste
1/8 tsp each ginger and black pepper
pinch cinnamon
½ cup white vinegar
½ tsp saffron

Directions:

Grind the breadcrumbs, spices and herbs (everything but the vinegar and saffron) together, in a mortar and pestle, food processor, or bowl with a heavy spoon. When you have mixed everything well together, warm the vinegar to medium heat in a small saucepan (not to boiling). Stir everything together until it has just begun to thicken. Add the saffron, stir together, and serve it.

a Traveling Basket Filled with Utensils

Sauces

a Man Planting a Tree

Verde Sawse (Green Sauce)   Traveling Dysshes

Savory Pies

(Suitable for entrees or side dishes, not deserts)

Because of their frugal habits, medieval cooks used pies in many meals, because they are a great way to use up leftovers. Pies are also a convenient and easy way to feed people, because they travel well and are their own serving dishes.

❖ Braun Pye (Pork Pie)

Caellyn FitzHugh, Forme of Cury, 1390, England and France
Serves 8-10 for a feast or potluck, 5-6 as a main dish. There are at least 5 braun (meat) recipes in Forme of Cury. Several describe using braun as either a stew-like consistency or in a jell, something like we use for an aspic. I suspect that Caellyn adapted that concept to put in a coffin, so as to better serve it out for feasts. I am particularly enamored of the description in this particular section of how to get the jellied meat out of the "vessel" – it sounds just like instructions for turning out a gelatin mold.

Original (one of them):

Take fresch braun (meat), boyle hit in fayre watyr till it be tendur. Blaunche almondys; greynd hem, draw hem up with the same broth and a perty of wyn, as hote as thu may. Than make thi milke hote, & do thy brawn in a streynour hot, and draw hit with the mylke hott. Do therto sygure a grete dele, & vynegar. Set hit on the fyre; boyle hit. Salt hit; do hit in another vessel. When it is cold, yf thu may mowght have it out, chaufe the vessel without wythe hotte water or ayenst the fyre.

Ingredients:

2 lb pork, uncooked, diced in ½" pieces
2 tsp sage leaves
1/2 cup ground almonds
1/2 tsp each salt, freshly ground pepper
1/2 tsp ground ginger
1/2 tsp ground cloves
1 cup raisins
2 onions, chopped
pork or veal bones
pastry for a coffin 6" or 8"

Savory Pies 55

Directions:

Make a broth by boiling the bones, almonds, onions and salt in 3 cups of water. Let it simmer for about an hour. Skim off the fat; boil until the liquid reduces to about 1 cup.

Mix the pork, ginger, cloves, salt, pepper and raisins well. Pack into the uncooked coffin.

Cover, being sure to leave a 1" vent hole in the center of the pie. Decorate the cover with small pastry cutouts of pigs, flowers, etc.

Bake for 15 minutes at 425 degrees F., remove the springform, reduce heat to 350, brush outside of crust with egg and water, and cook for 45 minutes more. Remove from oven.

Pour hot broth into the vent hole slowly, filling the (hot) pie. Serve hot or cold. If you choose to serve it cold, be sure you chill it thoroughly before serving.

a Swineherd Feeding Acorns to His Pigs

Braun Pye (Pork Pie) Traveling Dysshes

❖ Pyes of Chiken (Chicken Pie)

Jehanne de St. Brieuc, Forme of Cury, 1390, England and France
Jehanne extrapolated this recipe from the ones below and another recipe
called "Pyes of Capon, Flesch, and Fesauntez". Serves 8-10 for a feast or
potluck, 4 as a main dish. This is one of Siobhan's favorite pies, as it stores and
travels well, and always gets rave reviews from feasters.

Originals:

*To bake Chickins. Season them with cloves, mace, sinamon ginger, and
some pepper, so put them into your coffin, and put therto corance dates Prunes,
and sweet Butter, or els Marow, and when they be halfe baked, put in some sirup
of vergious, and some sugar, shake them togither and set them into the oven
again. Bake Sparowes, Larkes, or any kinde of small birds, calves feet or
sheepes tunges after the same manner.*
  *To make a Chickin Pye. Scalde the Chickins, draw them, and pull out the
brest bones, then season them with cloves and mace, Pepper and Salte, and if
you have them grapes, or gooseberies: when you have so doon, make paste of
fine flower, and put in your Chickins, and set them in the Oven, then boyle foure
Egs hard, then take the yolks and strain them with vergious, and put Sugar
thereto and put it into your Chicken pye when it is half baked, and when it is
ready to be served in, annoint it over with butter, Sugar & rosewater, then put it
into the oven til you serve them in.*
  *To bake Chickins without fruit. Season your Chickins with cloves, mace
and pepper, lay them into your paste with sweet butter, gooseberies, sugar and
whole mace. And when they be well baked, put therto vergious, yolkes of egges
strained, shake them togither and set them into the Oven againe. (from A Book
of Cookrye, 1591.)*

Ingredients:

1 lb boned cooked chicken, chopped into 1" pieces (When making a large
  number of these, Siobhan buys the individually frozen and "ice coated"
  boneless, skinless thighs" and cook them together.)
1 Tbsp melted butter
½ cup raisins or currants
½ tsp mace
2 tsp salt
1 tsp cinnamon
½ cup white wine
¼ cup chicken broth
2 eggs, slightly beaten
pastry for a coffin 6" or 8"

Savory Pies

Directions:

Mix all ingredients except the eggs and pastry and allow to steep together for 15 minutes. Add the eggs, mix well, and pack the coffin.

Cover, decorating the lid with chickens and other decorative pastry cutouts. Make sure you include several slits in the lid in the design.

Bake at 425 degrees F. for 15 minutes, remove the springform, reduce heat to 350, brush coffin with egg and water, and cook for 45 minutes more.

a Fowler Catching Birds in a Net

❖ Grete Pye (Beef, Chicken, & Hard Boiled Egg Pie)

Jehanne de St. Brieuc, Forme of Cury, 1390, England, and France

Putting this together can be a challenge, but it's well worth the effort when you cut into it and reveal the concentric rings of ingredients. The recipe has been simplified to make it easier to prepare for a feast. If you like, use as many meats as are described in the recipe. Serves 8-10 for feast or a potluck, 4 as a main dish.

Original:

Take good befe and sethe therwith porke, wele, or venison, hewn small. Do therto | pooudyr of pepyr, canell, poudyr of clovis, gynger, and mynsed datys, yf thu wilte, & and reysons of coraunce; & medyll hit with venygger, saffron, & salt, and take hit in thy mouth, yf it be welle sesond. Than couch hit in large cofyns, & close yn capons or fesauntez hole, or yf thu wilte, cut hit in pecys. Colour hem well with safron, & put theryn othir wylde foule, what thu wilt, & plant hit with half yolkes of eyron, & stre on clovis, macys, and datys mynsyd, corance, and quibibis. Close hem and bake hem long and sokyngly, & serve hem forth with the first cource.

Ingredients:

1 ½ lb ground beef or stew beef that has been shredded
½ tsp salt
¼ tsp pepper
1/8 tsp each cinnamon, ground cloves, ginger
¼ cup chicken broth
2 cups cooked diced chicken
4 dates, chopped
¼ cup currants
½ tsp cinnamon
¼ tsp each nutmeg, mace
2 hard boiled eggs, peeled
pastry for a coffin 6" or 8"

Directions:

In a small bowl, mix the beef, salt and pepper. Steep for 15 minutes. While the beef is spicing, in a second bowl, mix the chicken broth, dates, currants, and spices. Pack the beef into the coffin, tightly around the entire outer edge of the coffin, leaving a hole in the center for the chicken and eggs. Layer the chicken into the hole, leaving a space in the center for the eggs. Put the eggs in the center, whole.

Cover; decorate with cows, chickens, and other appropriate pastry cutouts. Bake for 15 minutes at 450 degrees, remove the springform, reduce heat to 350, brush with egg and water, and cook for 45-55 minutes more.

❖ Pygge in a Coffin (Ham Pie)

Caellyn FitzHugh, Forme of Cury, 1390, England and France and A Book of Cookrye, London, 1591

Caellyn synthesized this recipe from several sources, and I've listed one of the originals below. The one listed below is sweeter than Caellyn's version. If you use a canned ham, you can make an interestingly shaped coffin to go around the ham. The precooked hams sold at Easter are particularly convenient for this dish, even though the texture and curing are modern rather than anything seen in period.

Serves 10 - 12 for a feast or potluck, 8 as a main dish.

Original:

To bake a Pig like a Fawne: *Fley him when he is in the haire, season it with pepper and salt, mustard, Cloves and mace, take Claret wine, Vergious, Rosewater, Sinamon, Ginger and Sugar, boyle them togither, laye your Pig flat*

Savory Pies

like a Fawne or a Kidde, and put your sirup unto it and sweet butter, and so bake it leisurely.

Ingredients:

2-3 lbs precooked boneless ham, round
6 oz Dijon honey-mustard sauce or "country ground" Dijon mustard
½ tsp ginger
½ tsp mace
1/8 tsp ground cloves
2 Tbsp white wine
coffin for a pastry 8"-10" in diameter (or to fit the canned ham tin)

Directions:

Mix the mustard, spices, and wine together. While they are steeping together, make the coffin. Spread a layer of the mustard mixture in the bottom and on the sides of the coffin.

Put the ham in the coffin. If the ham is too tall, cut off the excess, spread with mustard mixture, and pack in around the edges. (You want to pack the coffin as tightly as possible.)

Spread the remaining mustard on the top of the ham. Be lavish. Use all of it.

Cover the coffin and decorate appropriately. ***Do Not*** make any slits or holes in the top of the coffin.

Bake for 15 minutes at 425 degrees F., remove the springform, reduce heat to 350, brush with egg and water, and cook for 30 minutes more.

Serve hot or cold.

a Boar

Pygge in a Coffin (Ham Pie)   Traveling Dysshes

❖ Auter Tartus (Tart of Cheese)

Siobhan fidhleir, Two Fifteenth-Century Cookery-Books, 1430-1450, England and France

Siobhan f. has added eggs to increase the protein content in this essentially vegetarian dish. Leave them out if you wish to hew more closely to the original recipe. Serves 8 for a potluck, 4 as a main dish.

Original:

Take faire nessh chese that is buttry, and par hit, grynd hit in a morter, caste thereto faire creme and grind hit tigidre; temper hit with goode mylke, that hit be no thikker then rawe creme, and cast therto a litul salt if nede be; and thi cheese be salte, caste therto neuer a dele; colour hit with saffron; then make a large coffyn of faire paste, & lete the brinkes be rered more then an enche of hegh; lete the coffyn harden in the oven; then take it oute, put gobettes of butter in the bothom thereof, And caste the stuffe there-to and cast peces of buttur there-yppon, and sette in the oven with-oute lydde, and lete bake ynouwe, and then cast sugur thereon, and serue it forth. And if thou wilte, let him haue a lydde; but then thi stuff must be as thikke as Mortrews.

Ingredients:

1 lb white cheese, grated (use Mexican queso fresco, as being close to "chese
    newe")
1 cup cream
1 cup half-and-half
pinch saffron
2 eggs beaten
2 each 8" pastry shells

Directions:

Process the cheese, milkstuffs, and eggs in a food processor until smooth. Prebake the pastry shells at 425 degrees F. for 18 minutes, remove shells from oven, reduce heat to 325, fill shells with filling (as the medieval original indicates, the filling puffs up, so don't overfill), and bake for 30 minutes.

Savory Pies

❖ How to make Tartes of Spinage

Siobhan Medhbh, A Book of Cookrye, London, 1591)
Serves 8 at a feast, 4 as a main dish.

Original:

Boyle your Spinage very tender, and three or foure apples with it, and when it is very tender, straine it through a faire cloth, and then season it with the yolk of an egge, Sugar, Sinamon, and Ginger.

Ingredients:

Pie shell for a 8" single pie
½ lb. baby spinach, washed (or two boxes of frozen spinach)
3 apples, peeled, cored, and cut into chunks
1 egg yolk, beaten until glossy
2 Tbsp. sugar
1 tsp. cinnamon
1 tsp. grated ginger (1/4 tsp. dried ground ginger)

Directions:

Preheat your oven to 350 o F. In a saucepan, place the cut apples and the washed greens. Fill with water to just cover the spinach (hold it down gently with your hand if it floats too much), and bring to a boil. When the greens are wilted (some may prefer to let their spinach cook a little longer) and the apples are soft, drain the liquid. Mix in the egg and spices, pour into the pie shell, and bake for 30-40 minutes., until the crust is browned and the filling looks firm. Serve hot or cold.

a Woman
Baking Bread

❖ Tart de Bry (Brie Tart)

Jehanne de St. Brieuc, Forme of Cury, 1390, England and France

For those of us who love brie, this is a real treat. It keeps well for tournaments, and can be served warm or cold. It's delightfully fragrant while cooking, too. Serves 6-8 at a feast, 4-5 as a main dish.

Original:

Take a crust inch deep in a trap. Take yolks of ayren raw and cheese ruayn1 and medle it and the yolks together and do thereto powder ginger, sugar, saffron, and salt. Do it in a trap, bake it and serve it forth.

Ingredients:

Pastry for a covered 9" pie shell
3 eggs, beaten
5 oz brie cheese
¼ tsp salt
¼ tsp ground ginger
½ tsp sugar
2-3 threads saffron

Directions:

Preheat the oven to 375°F. Make your pie shell, holding pastry for the cover in reserve. Chop the cheese into small bits, and stir together with the beaten eggs and spices. Cover the pie with the reserved pastry and bake for 15-20 minutes.

Men Making Cheese

Savory Pies

❖ To Make a Tarte of Spinnage (Spinach Pie) or of Wheate Leaves or of Colewortes
Cordelia Toser, The Good Hus-wives Jewell, 1596
This sauce is a good accompaniment for roast venison or goose.

Original:
Take three handfull of Spinnage, boile it in faire water, when it is boyled, put away the water from it and put the spinnage in a stone morter, grind it smal with two dishes of butter melted, and foure rawe eggs all to beaten, then straine it and season it with suger, Sinamon and ginger, and lay it in your Coffin, when it is hardened in the oven, then bake it, and when it is enough, serve it upon a faire dish, and cast upon it Suger and Biskets.

Ingredients:
20 oz frozen chopped spinach
2 Tbsp melted butter
6 large eggs,
1 Tbsp sugar
2 tsp ground cinnamon
2 tsp ginger, ground
1 uncooked pie crust 9"

Directions:
Preheat oven to 350 degrees F. Thaw spinach. Beat eggs in a large bowl until uniform, then mix in the other ingredients. Pour mixture into pie shell and bake 40 to 45 minutes. Remove pie from oven and sprinkle 1 more spoonful of sugar over it. Cool before cutting into slices.

a Picnic for Nobles

Fruits

❖ Chardewardon (Pear Sauce)

Katerine, Two Fifteenth-Century Cookery-Books, Manuscript Harleian 279, Potage Dyvers xxxiv, page 12; 1430, England

Katerine says, "This is pear sauce, subtle and wonderful. They also did applesauce ("applemoy," "applemoise"), but I like this better. If I want a medieval applesauce I do this, but replace the pears by cooking apples. But the original is so good I rarely stray from it. But remember – cooking pears! Not eating pears!"

Serves 4 if they take it as a relish or very small side dish. Serves 2 with normal appetites.

Original:

Take Pere Wardonys, an sethe hem in wyne or fayre water; than take an grynd in a morter, an draw hem thorwe a straynoure wyth-owte ony lycoure, an put hem in a potte with Sugre and clarifyd hony, an Canel y-now, an lete hem boyle; than take it fro the fyre, an let kele, an caste ther-to zolkys of Raw eyroun, tylle it be thikke; & caste ther-to pouder Gyngere y-now, an serue it in manere of Fyshhe; and zif if it be in lente, lef the zolkys of Eyroun, & lat the remenaunt boyle so longe tylle it be thikke, as thow it had be temperyd with the zolkys, in the manner of charde quynce; an so serue hem in manner of Rys.

Ingredients:

4 bosc pears
½ tsp cinnamon
1 cup dry white wine
1 cup water
1 egg yolk (raw)
1 Tbsp sugar
1 Tbsp honey
¼ tsp ginger

Directions:

Peel and core pears. Boil in wine and water 25 minutes, until the pears are soft and most of the liquid has been absorbed or boiled off. Drain, then blend until smooth.

Add remaining ingredients.

Fruits   65

❖ Bolas/Bullace/Bullyce (Dark Plums)

Siobhan Medhbh, Two Fifteenth-Century Cookery Books (Harleian MS 279)

This is a dish that, while it has many steps, is delightful to look at and to eat. It rivals the best of the presentation dishes seen in restaurants, and has a pleasant tart flavor. Even though it was completely new to the feast at which we served it at, there were no leftovers returned to the kitchen!

Original:

Take fayre Bolasse, wasshe hem clene, & in Wyne boyle hem þat þe be but skaldyd bywese, & boyle hem alle to pomppe, & draw hem þorw a straynoure, & a-lye hem with flower of Rys, & make it chargeaunt, & do it to þe fyre, & boyle it; take it of, & do þer-to white Sygrem gyngere, Clowys, Maces, Canelle, & stere it wyl to-gederys: þanne take datis, & wasshe hem clene, & pyke owt þe Stonys, & fylle hem fulle of blaunche pwudere: þan take þe Stalke of þe Perys, take þe Bolas, & ley .iij. lechys in a dysshe, & sette þin preys þere-yn.

Ingredients:

½ lb red plums, washed and pitted
1 cup red wine or burgundy
1 tsp rice flour
1 ripe, firm pear, halved and cored
3 dates, pitted and halved lengthwise
2 Tblsp sugar
1 tsp ginger powder
1/8 tsp clove
½ tsp mace
1 tsp cinnamon

Directions:

Put plums and ½ cup red wine in a covered pot. Boil; cook until the plums turn to pulp. Remove from heat.

Strain the wine and plums through a strainer into a pot. Add rice flour and stir. Re-heat, stirring steadily until the mixture thickens slightly. Add spices and stir until the mixture is as thick as liquid jelly.

Remove from heat, pour into a shallow dish and set aside.

Cook the pear in ½ cup red wine until it is fork tender. Remove, drain, slice into six slices. Arrange on the dish with the plum sauce.

Take the six date pieces, sprinkle with white powder, and arrange with the sauce and pears. Serve cold.

66   Fruits

a Portable Baking Overn

Traveling Dysshes   Bolas/Bullace/Bullyce (Dark Plums)

Vegetables 67

Vegetables

❖ Salat (Green Salad)

Everyone, Forme of Cury #78, 1390, England and France

This is a green salad much like we are used to, only with more onion-related components. This is not the garden salad served at restaurants – there are no carrots, radishes, or tomatoes. If you care about such things, remember that this is a late spring and summer dish only, as there were no ways to transport fresh greens in the dead of winter from more tropical growing areas.

You should be able to fill one very large salad bowl with this salad.

Original:

Take persel, sawge, grene garlek, chibolles, oynouns, leek, borage, myntes, porrettes, fenel, and toun cressis, rew, rosemarye, purslarey; lave and waishche hem clene. Pike hem. Plum hem small with thyn honde, and myng hem wel with rawe oile; laye on vyneger and salt, and serue it forth.

Ingredients:

Greens: use an assortment of spinach, leaf lettuce, borage, beet tops, turnip
    greens, mustard, etc. [Do not use iceberg, boston, or romaine lettuce.]
1 Tbsp each fresh herbs: chopped parsley, sage, mint leaves, dill, fennel, savory,
    etc. (Find as many of these as you can fresh: if you must use dried, use 1 tsp
    each)
2 bunches scallions, sliced thin. Use the tops and the bulbs.
1 clove of garlic minced fine
3 small or 1 large leek, well washed and sliced into thin rings
½ cup olive oil
¼ cup vinegar
1 ½ tsp salt

Directions:

Wash the greens and tear them small. Drain on paper towels or in a salad spinner. Put in a large salad bowl and toss with herbs, leeks, scallions, oil, and garlic. (If you have cut the ingredients fine enough, they will not fall to the bottom of the bowl.)

Just before serving out, mix the vinegar and salt. Pour over the salad and toss well.

Salat (Green Salad)   Traveling Dysshes

❖ Rape Armate (Turnip Cake, or Armoured Turnips)

Siobhan fidhleir, Platina, book 8, 1475, Italy
Rapunzel, look out. As unusual as this dish sounds, it's quite popular.
Serves 8 as a side dish or dessert.

Original:

Cut up turnips that have been either boiled or cooked under the ashes. Likewise do the same with rich cheese, not too ripe. These should be smaller morsels than the turnips, though. In a pan greased with butter or liquamen, make a layer of cheese first, then a layer of turnips, and so on, all the while pouring in spice and some butter, from time to time. This dish is quickly cooked and should be eaten quickly, too.

Ingredients:

2 lb large white turnips
¼-1/3 cup sugar
2 ½ tsp ground cinnamon
1 ½ tsp pepper, ground fine
½ tsp mace
½ tsp ground cloves
1 ¼ soft white cheese, thinly sliced

Directions:

Boil the unpeeled turnips in water to cover until just tender (15-30 minutes). Drain, cool, and peel. Cut them into ¼ inch slices. Mix the sugar with the spices.

Preheat the oven to 375 degrees F.

Thickly butter a 9" square pan and arrange a layer of turnips in the bottom.

Add a layer of cheese overlapping on top; sprinkle with some of the sugar mixture. Continue until the ingredients are all used up, ending with a layer of cheese. [Don't you just love instructions like that?]

Bake the dish in the heated oven until the top is browned (30-35 minutes). Turn out onto a platter, and cut into wedges or squares for serving. As a dessert it can be served hot or cold. As a side dish, it is best served hot.

Vegetables

❖ Caboches in Potage (Cabbage in Broth)

Siobhan fidhleir, Forme of Cury, 1390, England and France
This recipe as redacted is totally vegan. If you wish, you can use chicken broth instead. Serves 6-8 at a potluck, 4-5 as a soup with a main dish.

Original:

Take caboches and quarter hem, and seethe hem in gode broth with oynouns ymynced and the whyte of lekes yslyt and ycorue smale. And do therto safroun & salt, and force it with powdour douce.

Ingredients:

1 head cabbage, cored and quartered
2 chopped onions
2 chopped leeks
8 cups vegetable broth
2 tsp salt
¼ tsp each cinnamon, sugar, cardamom, galingale
pinch saffron

Directions:

Heat a little oil in the soup pot and cook onions until translucent. Add broth, bring to a boil. Then add cabbage, leeks and spices, and cook until the cabbage is done to your liking.

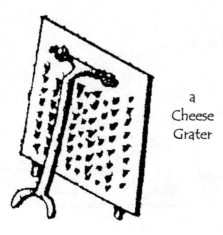

a Cheese Grater

Caboches in Potage (Cabbage in Broth)   Traveling Dysshes

❖ Funges (Mushrooms)

Jehanne, Forme of Cury, 1390, England and France

Serves 6 at a potluck, 3 as a side dish or appetizer. Fewer if the cooks like mushrooms.

Original:

Take Funges and pare hem clene and dyce hem. Take Leke and shred hem smal and do hym to seethe in gode broth. Color hit with safroun and do thinne powdour forte.

Ingredients:

1 lb mushrooms, washed and sliced thick
1 leek, washed and shredded fine
1 cup broth, preferably Chicken although beef will do (vegetarian broth will make this a totally vegan dish)
1/8 tsp each ginger, mace, cardamom, white pepper, cubeb
salt to taste
pinch of saffron (optional)

Directions:

Mix the broth and spices (including the saffron) together; heat to boiling. Add the mushrooms and leeks and reduce the heat to low. Simmer for 10 minutes (or until the mushrooms are cooked soft enough for your taste). Salt to taste. If you wish to make this into mushroom soup, triple the broth. Serve over slices of toast.

a Busy Kitchen

Vegetables   71

❖ A Grand Sallet of Beets, Currants & Greens
(Greens & Beet Salad)

Siobhan Medhbh, from Robert May, The Accomplisht Cook, England, 1604.

This is a very cool example of arranged salads, of which Robert May is an absolute master. This one is easy and decorative, and very nice in hot weather. Serves 10.

Original:

Take the youngest and smallest leaves of spinage, the smallest also of sorrel, well washed currans, and red beets round the center being finely carved, oyl and vinegar, and the dish garnished with lemon and beets.

Ingredients:

3 cups fresh baby spinach, washed
2 cups small sorrel leaves, washed
½ cup currants
8 beets, cooked, peeled and sliced (a small can of cooked beets can be
    substituted, drained and rinsed.)
2 lemons, sliced thinly
olive oil and red wine vinegar to taste (for me, ¼ cup oil and ½ cup vinegar)

Directions:

Taking small petits fours or other decorative cookie cutters, cut your beets into decorative shapes. Set aside the beet remnants. Very thinly slice the lemons, discarding the ends. Refrigerate until needed in a closed container.

Make sure the spinach and sorrel are well washed, as they can be very gritty. Pat dry, and tear into bits in a large bowl. Add currants, oil, vinegar, and beet slivers, and toss well.

Arrange the salad on a platter with a lip, or a large shallow bowl. Just before you serve it out, arrange the decorative beets and lemon slices on the top of the greens. Serve cold.

A Grand Sallet of Beets, Currants & Greens   Traveling Dysshes

❖ Cress in Lent with Milk of Almonds

Siobhan Medhbh, Le Menagier.
This is another vegetarian dish. Serves 8.

Original:

Take your cress and parboil it with a handful of chopped beet leaves, and fry them in oil, then put to boil in milk of almonds ; and when it is not Lent, fry in lard and butter until cooked, then moisten with meat stock; or with cheese, and adjust it carefully, for it will brown. Anyway, if you add parsley, it does not have to be blanched.

Ingredients:

2/3 lb spinach or watercress
½ cup beet leaves or chard or turnip tops
1 Tbsp olive oil or butter
½ cup almond milk
1 ounce of parsley
pinch salt

Directions:

Chop the cress and other greens. Dump them into boiling water, let the water come back to a boil, then drain them (about 2 minutes total in water). Heat oil or lard or butter in a skillet, add drained greens (and chopped parsley if you are using parsley). Stir fry for about 3 minutes. For Lenten version, add almond milk, let boil with greens about a minute. For fish-day version, add cheese, chopped up and stir until cheese is melted into the greens. For meat-day version, add meat stock and cook down 2-3 minutes. Add salt, serve.

a Sugar Grater

Vegetables   73

❖ A dysshe of Artichokes (Baked Artichokes)

Siobhan Medhbh, Hugh Platt, The Accomplisht Ladys Delight
Serves 6-8

Original:

Take the bottoms of six Artichoaks Boyled very tender, put them in a dish, and some Vinegar over them. Season them with Ginger and Sugar, a little Mace Whole, and put them in a Coffin of Paste. When you lay them in, lay some Marrow and Dates slices, and a few Raisons of the Sun in the bottom with a good store of butter. When it is half baked, take a Gill of Sack, being boyled first with Sugar and a peel of Orange. Put it into the Pye, and set it in the oven again, till you use it.

Ingredients:

Small Coffin (6" springform) (see page 40)
6 artichoke bottoms (the tops and stickers cut off)
½ tsp salt
½ tsp mace
1 tsp sugar
½ tsp ground ginger
1 Tbsp vinegar
2 Tbs melted butter
2 Tbsp. beef marrow
¼ cup raisins
¼ cup dates, sliced
½ C dry sherry
1 Tbsp. sugar
Sliver of orange peel, ½" by 2"

Directions:

Boil the Artichokes until they are very tender. Put them in a casserole, and sprinkle the vinegar, sugar, ginger, and mace. Let them sit while you make a coffin.

On the bottom of the coffin, spread the butter, raisins, dates, and marrow. Close, cover, and decorate, leaving a small hole in the top of the coffin. Bake according to the directions on page 40.

While the pie is baking, make the sherry sauce: in a heavy-bottomed pan, warm the sherry with the sugar and orange peel. Let it just come to a boil. (Alternately, in a Pyrex® or microwave-safe measuring cup or bowl, heat the sherry, sugar, and peel for 1:30 minutes on High.) About 10 minutes after you

A dysshe of Artichokes (Baked Artichokes)   Traveling Dysshes

remove the springform, take the pie out of the oven, and pour the sherry mixture into the pie through the hole. Serve out hot.

❖ Benes y-Fride   (Fried Beans)

Siobhan Medhbh, Forme of Cury, 1390, England and France

Another good potluck dish. This can also be prepared easily on-site in a standard frying pan.

Serves 6 at a potluck, 3 as a main dish or side dish.

Original:

Take benes and seth hem almost til they bersten. Take and wryng out the water clene. Do therto onyouns ysod and ymynced, and garlec therwith; frye hem in oile othr in grece, & do therto powdour douce, & serue it forth.

Ingredients:

1 onion, chopped fine
1 clove garlic, finely chopped
¼ cup oil
¼ tsp ginger
½ tsp cinnamon
¼ tsp nutmeg
6 oz of northern beans, cooked

Directions:

Fry the onions in the oil with the garlic, spices, and seasonings. Stir in the cooked beans and mix thoroughly.

Another day, you can bake these in a casserole until reheated.

a Casserole

Vegetables   75

❖ Frumenty (Wheat & Milk Pottage)

Siobhan Medhbh, An Ordinance of Pottage.

Frumenty is, at base, porridge. It's a delightful combination of grains and textures, which accompanies game very well. It's great reheated for breakfast, too. Serves 8.

Original:

To make furmenty; Nym clene wete & bray it in a morter well, (th)at (th)e holys gon al of, & seyt yt til it breste & nym it up & lat it kele. And nym fayre fresch bro(th) and swete mylk of almandys or swete mylk of kyne and temper yt al & nym (th)e (y)olks of eyren & saffron & do therto. Boyle it a lityl & set yt down & messe yt forth yth fat venysoun & fresch motoun.

Ingredients:

3 cups wheat berries (I use red, but you can use spring berries, which are softer)
6 cups water
3 cups milk
¼ tsp salt
1 egg yolk
pinch saffron

Directions:

Bring the wheat berries to a boil in the water, then let them sit for half an hour. Bring them back to a boil and cook them until they soften and burst (this could be as little as 10 minutes, or as long as a half hour. Stir frequently if not constantly, and don't let it burn on the bottom. While the wheat is cooking, warm the milk (don't boil it). Using a whisk, mix the egg-yolk and then the salt into the milk.

When the berries are softened, take them off the heat. Drain off the water, reserving 2-3 cups. Stir in the warm milk and egg mixture, with a little of the reserved water to make it smooth. Cook over low heat until it resembles porridge or cream of wheat. Be careful not to let it scorch. If you need to hold it before serving it, use a crock pot or double boiler.

Some people like this with sugar, which is probably a modern interpretation. "Sweet milk" means fresh milk, as opposed to buttermilk or sour milk.

❖ Mustard Greens

Cariadoc and Elizabeth, Anthimus, as listed in the Miscellany.

Original:

Mustard greens are good, boiled in salt and oil. They should be eaten either cooked on the coals or with bacon, and vinegar to suit the taste should be put in while they are cooking.

Ingredients:

- 1 ¼ lb mustard greens (including smaller stems)
- 1 tsp salt
- 3 Tblsp oil
- 4 slices bacon
- 4 tsp vinegar

Directions:

Wash mustard greens. Boil stems two minutes, then add leaves, boil 6 more minutes and drain. Fry bacon (6 minutes in microwave). Heat oil, add greens and stir, then add salt and cook five minutes. Crumble bacon and put over greens with vinegar. Stir it all up and cook another 3 minutes.

a Woman Cutting Leeks

Vegetables

❖ Buttered Marrows

Siobhan Medhbh, Two Fifteenth-Century Cookery Books

This recipe is an extrapolation. In *Le Menagier* we have the instruction that veggies can be cooked in clene water and with a little sweet butter. *Le Viandier de Taillevant* says of cooked vegetables "women are experts with these and anyone knows how to do them." So extrapolating from buttered greens and boiled roots, Siobhan created this dish.

Marrows are root veggies. In England they have a green vegetable called a marrow, which looks and tastes like (and may well be) a large zucchini. One modern way to prepare it is to cut it in half lengthwise, scoop out the seeds, stuff it with a meat filling and bake. Siobhan's favorite mix is carrots and rutabagas; you can choose your own.

Serves 8 at a potluck, 5 as a side dish.

Original:

Take al manor of good herbes that thou may gete, and do bi ham as is forsaid; putte hem on the fire with faire water; put ther-to clarefied buttur a grete quantite. Whan thei ben boyled ynough, salt hem; late none otemele come ther-in. Dise brede small in disshes, and powre on the wortes, and serue hem forth.(Le Menagier)

Ingredients:

5 carrots
the same number of rutabagas, less one
3 Tbsp butter, cut in tiny pieces
salt and pepper to taste

Directions:

Peel the marrows and cut in small pieces. Boil until they are tender. Mash together until they resemble mashed potatoes (an old-fashioned potato masher does marvelously if you have no electricity). Mix in the butter, salt and pepper, and serve piping hot.

❖ Butterd Worts (Buttered Greens)

Siobhan fidhleir, Two Fifteenth-Century Cookery-Books, Harleian MS. 4016, 1450, England and France

Buttered worts are leaves of various greens. We don't know how cooked the author means, as he says "whan thei ben boyled enough, salt hem." Heiatt and Butler [*Pleyn Delit*] recommend blanching the greens and not cooking them overmuch. Do what seems best to you.

Because this dish is cooked with water and not broth, it is a vegetarian dish. Serves 10-12 at a potluck, 8 as a side dish.

Original:

Take all manner of good herbes that thou may gete, and do by ham as is foresaid; putte hem on the fire with faire water; put here-to clarefied buttur a grete quantite. Whan thei ben boyled enough, salt hem; late none otemele come herein. Dise brede small in disshes, and powre on the wortes, and serue hem forth.

Ingredients:

2-3 lbs mixed greens (cabbage leaves, beet greens, borage, turnip tops, parsley, leeks, mustard, spinach: whatever suits your fancy and is available in season. Frozen greens don't make it in this dish.)
3 onions or leeks
2-4 tsp butter (more if you desire) or 4 tsp of ghee
6 slices of bread, diced and toasted (or about 2 cups plain croutons)

Directions:

Wash the greens well. Some greens require 4 rinses to get all the grit out. The traditional southern method of washing greens is to put the greens in the sink, fill the sink with water, and stir vigorously with your hands while the grit falls to the bottom. Lift out the greens, let the grit go down the drain, and repeat until no more grit comes out. (If you are doing this at a camping event, it's probably best to wash the greens at home. Otherwise, camp near the water source.)

Boil a large pot of salted water. Blanch the greens and onions together in the salted water for 2-4 minutes. (The easiest way to do this is to use one of those combination pasta and boiling pans, and put the greens in the pasta basket. Failing that, put a metal colander in the pot and blanch the greens in the colander. After 2-4 minutes, lift the basket or colander out, and the greens come with.)

Chop the greens and onions or leeks to medium size. Put in a pan with the butter and ¾ cup water; stir well, cover, and let rest over low heat for 5 minutes. Salt to taste; toss with the bread cubes and serve.

Vegetables 79

an Illustration of Trees in a Garden

Butterd Worts (Buttered Greens) — Traveling Dysshes

Cheese & Eggs

Cheese and Eggs are probably the most ubiquitous meal on the planet, and it's entirely reasonable that every culture that eats these two foods combines them. Cheese is an easy way to store the goodness of milk, by processing it into cheese. Eggs can be eaten fresh, or made to travel well by hard-boiling them. They are easy to add to your store of foods at an event, and can be served out at almost any meal.

❖ Loseyns (Cheese Lasagne)

Siobhan Medhbh, Forme of Cury #78, 1390, England and France

Loseyns (pronounced "lozenges or "lah-sayns") gets its name from the distinctive lozenge-shaped pattern in which you cut it before serving. Like its cousin Macrows, this is one of the most familiar of medieval foods. Serves 8 at a potluck, 4-5 as a main dish.

Original:

Take good broth and do in an erthen pot. Take flour of payndemayn and make thereof past with water, and seeth it in the broth. Take chese ruayn grated and lay it in dishes with powdour douce, and lay theron loseynss isode at hool as thou might, and aboe all powdour and chese; and so twyse or thryse, and serue it forth.

Ingredients:

1 lb. box of lasagna noodles (If you are good at making your own pasta, go for it!)
2 cups beef or chicken broth (optional: vegetarians can use water to cook the noodles)
1 lb grated cheese (I use a mix of cheddar, parmesan, mozzarella, or others)
4 tsp butter
½ cup milk
½ cup sugar
¼ tsp ginger
¼ tsp mace

Directions:

Boil the noodles in the broth (or water). While that is cooking, put the cheese in a big bowl. Mix in the milk, sugar and spices. Let it sit while the noodles cook.

Drain the noodles. Dot the bottom of a loaf (or 8" x 8" square) pan with butter. Put in a layer of noodles, then a layer of cheese, then a layer of noodles, alternating until the pan is filled. Save enough cheese to cover the top layer of noodles.

Cook at 350 degrees F. for 20 minutes or until the top begins to bubble and turn lightly golden. Remove from heat; let sit for 5 minutes, then cut in a diamond pattern. Serve! (Some people like these cold, but they disappear in moments when piping hot from the oven.)

Two Women Making Noodles

❖ Stuffed Tubes (Fried Cheese)

Siobhan Medhbh, Le Menagier, 1393, Paris

Ever wonder who came up with the idea of deep-fried mozzarella? Wasn't TGIF or any other modern restaurant chain—it was our friends in France in the 14th century. But beware! This is a tricky dish — if the fat is too cool, leaving them in long enough to get brown melts the cheese. If too hot, the outside gets black and the cheese stays hard. So, you have to experiment and watch the temperature of your fat.

Original:

If you wish to make some stuffed tubes, have good harvest cheese in strips as fat as your finger. Coat them in the batter for small crisps, insert them into your hot lard, and keep them from burning. When they are dry and yellowish, set them out with crisps.

Ingredients:

½ lb mozzarella or other soft white cheese (can also use cheddar)
oil
The recipe for the batter is "Cryspes", page 37

Directions:

Cut the cheese into strips. Heat vegetable oil in a deep skillet (or wok) until a drop of batter cooks brown almost immediately. Coat in the batter. Gently put in the oil; fry until golden brown. Remove, and serve immediately!

an Egg Pan

Cheese & Eggs   83

❖ Longe Frutours (Fried Fresh Cheese)

Cordelia Toser, Harleian Ms. 4016, 1450

You may decide to serve this dish as dessert. Warning: do not taste this before you get it to the table, or it may not get there.

Serves 2-4.

Original:

Take Mylke and make faire croddes there-of in manner of chese al tendur, and take oute the way clene; then put hit in a faire boll, And take yolkes of egges, and white, and menge floure, and caste thereto a good quantite; and draw hit thorgh a streynoure into a faire vessell; then put hit in a faire pan, and fry hit a littul in faire grece, but lete not boyle; then take it oute, and ley on a faire borde, and kutte it in faire smale peces as thou list, And putte hem ayen into the panne until thei be browne; And then caste Sugur on hem, an serue hem forth.

Ingredients:

2 cups cottage cheese, small curd
1 large egg
1 cup flour
6 Tbsp butter
½ cup sugar (divided)

Directions:

Mix cottage cheese, egg, flour and 6 Tbsp sugar in bowl. Put 2 Tbsp butter in large skillet over medium low heat. Put half the cheese mixture in skillet and pat into a rectangle about ¼ inch thick. Cook until solid enough to turn over without breaking - about 15-20 minutes. At this point add another Tbsp butter.

When second surface is browned, remove patty from skillet and cook remaining half of cheese mixture in the same fashion.

Cut both patties into finger-shaped pieces, gently place them back in the skillet to brown the cut edges, then place on a serving platter. Sprinkle with remaining sugar and serve hot.

Longe Frutours (Fried Fresh Cheese)   Traveling Dysshes

❖ An Herbal Dish or Two of Eggs (Herbed Omelette)

Siobhan Medhbh, Le Menagier, 1393, Paris (translated by Janet Hinson, with amendments by David Friedman and Elizabeth Cook)

This is a lovely morning omlette, and easy to make, too. The directions on how to keep the cheese from burning and sticking to the pan are particularly charming. With energetic eaters, it will serve 4.

Original:

Take just two leaves of coq, and of rue less than half that or none at all, for remember that it is strong and bitter: of celery, tansy, mint and sage, no more than four leaves of each or less: of sweet marjoram a little more, more fennel, and yet more parsley; but of the leaves of white beet and beet, violet leaves, spinach, lettuce, and mother-of-sage, in equal amounts so that altogether you have two good handfuls: clean and wash in cold water, then rinse and remove all the water, and grind up two pieces of ginger; then put your herbs through the mortar two or three times, along with the said ginger, and grind up together. And then take sixteen well-beaten eggs, both yolks and whites, and grind and stir in the mortar along with what is already there, then divide in two, and make two thick omelettes which will be fried in the following manner: first you will heat your frying-pan thoroughly with oil, butter, or some such grease as you like, and when it is nice and hot all over, especially towards the handle, mix and pour your eggs into the pan and turn often with a flipper, then throw on some good grated cheese; and remember that it is done this way because if you grind the cheese with the herbs and eggs, when you put it in the pan to cook, the cheese on the underside would stick to the pan; and similarly with a cheese omelette if you mix the cheese with the eggs. So for this reason put the eggs in the pan first, and put the cheese on top, and then bring the edge of the egg over to cover: otherwise it will stick to the pan. And when your herbs are fried in the pan, you can give your herbal dish a square or round shape and eat it not too hot and not too cold.

Ingredients:

If you have fresh herbs:
2 leaves of Cock's Comb (also calledYellow Rattle Grass, Pennygrass)
1 sm leaf of rue
4 leaves each of celery, tansy, mint, and sage
6 leaves of marjoram
8 leaves of fennel
1 large stalk of parsley
2 pieces of fresh ginger root the size of your little finger

Cheese & Eggs

If you have dried herbs:
1/8 tsp. ground Cock's Comb
1/16 tsp. ground rue
1/8 tsp. dried celery leaves
1/8 tsp. dried mint leaves
1/8 tsp. dried tansy leaves
1/8 tsp. dried sage
¼ tsp. dried marjoram leaves
3/8 tsp. dried fennel
½ tsp. dried parsley flakes
1 tsp. ground ginger

Plus:
Baby Spinach, Beet leaves, violet leaves, and sage, to fill a 2-cup measure.
10 eggs, beaten
1 cup grated cheese
oil for the fry pan

Directions:

If using fresh herbs, wash and pat dry all the herbs. Wash and pat dry the greens (Spinach, beets, violet, sage). In a mortar, grind together all the fresh herbs, then add the greens and the ginger. (If you are using a food processor or blender, do not puree the leaves into a pulp; just chop them into tiny bits. The color and texture are part of the pleasure of the dish.)

Mix the eggs with the herbs, in the mortar or processor, and swirl together until well beaten. Divide the resulting mixture in half, reserving the second half for the second omlette.

Heat the skillet to medium, and pour in the eggs. Let them cook for a few minutes, then turn with a spatula or egg turner. Repeat several times until the eggs are cooked through but not brown and hard.

Sprinkle half the cheese onto the omlette, let it melt for a few minutes on the hot eggs, then slide the omlette onto a plate and serve.

Repeat the process for the second half of the mix.

a Kitchen Boy Catching Geese

An Herbal Dish or Two of Eggs (Herbed Omelette)   Traveling Dysshes

Fish

There's a story that you can't get SCA-folk to eat fish. One easy answer—try this recipe. You'll rarely get leftovers back in the kitchen!

❖ Salmon Roste in Sauce

Cordelia Toser, Two Fifteenth-Century Cookery-Books, 1430-1450, England and France

The sauce is quite vinegary, which is very typical of period sauces for fish. If you prefer a less puckery sauce, increase the wine and leave out the vinegar. The chyne is the spine, so the suggested cuts will have bones. I opted to avoid the bones and used fillet instead. Serves 5-6 as a main dish.

Original:

Take a Salmond, and cut him rounde, chyne and all, and rost the peces on a gredire; and take wyne, and pouder of Canell, and draw it thorgh a streynour; And take smale myced oynons, and caste there-to, and lete hem boyle; And then take vynegre, or vergeous, and pouder ginger, and cast there-to; and then ley the samon in a dissh, and cast the sirip thereon al hote, & serue it forth.

Ingredients:

1 ¾ lb salmon filet, skinned
¾ cup sweet white wine
¼ cup red wine vinegar
¾ cup chopped onions
¾ tsp cinnamon
¼ tsp ginger
salt to taste

Directions:

Place chopped onions, wine, vinegar and spices in a small saucepan. Cook uncovered on low heat until onions are softened, 20-30 minutes.

Skin (and de-bone) salmon, cut into serving size pieces, and place on ungreased baking pan, loosely keeping the fish shape. Broil at 400 degrees F. for 7 minutes. Remove fish from oven, turn pieces and reassemble fish shape. Broil for an additional 7 minutes (or a couple of minutes more if it's very thick).

Place cooked salmon on an oval platter, pour sauce over the fish, and serve.

Fish 87

Catching Fish in a Seine-net

Salmon Roste in Sauce · Traveling Dysshes

Poultry & Rabbit

Chicken is a perennial favorite — always a good choice on the menu. It's easy, and there are a lot of varieties of ways to cook it, whole, or in pieces, or in a pie. Plus, almost everyone who isn't a vegetarian eats chicken, so you can almost guarantee at least one dish everyone will eat!

❖ Sawse Madam (Goose [or Chicken] with Fruit Stuffing)

Siobhan Medhbh, Forme of Cury, 1390, England and France
This is a wonderful stuffing and sauce for chicken, duck, or goose.
Serves 8-10 at a potluck or feast, 5-6 as a main dish.

Original:

Take sawge, persel, ysope, and saueray, quinces and peeres, garleck and grapes, and fylle the gees therwith; and sowe the hole that no grece can come out, and roost hem wel, and kepe the grece that fallith therof. Take galyntyne and grece and do in a possynet. Whan the geese beeth rosted ynowh, take hem of and smyte hem on pecys, and take that that is withinne and do it in a possynet and put thereinne wyne, if it be to thyk; do therto powdour of galyngale, powdour douce, and salt and boyle the sawse, and dresse the gees in disshes and lay the sewe onward.

Ingredients:

5 lb bird
1 tsp each dried sage, parsley, hyssop (or mint), and savory
2 small pears, peeled, cored and chopped
2-3 quinces, peeled, cored and chopped
2 cloves garlic, minced fine
1 to 1 ½ cup seedless grapes
½ cup dry breadcrumbs
½ tsp cinnamon
¼ tsp galingale
½ cup wine vinegar
1/3 cup red wine
1 tsp salt (more or less to taste)

Poultry & Rabbit

Directions:

In a bowl mix the fruit, dried herbs and garlic. Stuff the bird with this mixture, and sew or skewer the opening shut. Roast on a rack in an open pan for 30 minutes per pound. Pour off the fat as it accumulates and set aside. (This much more critical for duck or goose than chicken.)

When the bird is cooking, soak the breadcrumbs in the vinegar. When the bird is done, mix together the breadcrumbs, remaining spices, wine and about 1/8 cup of the drippings from the bird. Whisk smooth, salt to taste.

Pour over the bird; serve it forth.

❖ Chike Endored (Gilded Chicken)

Siobhan Medhbh, Pleyn Delit, 2nd edition, Heiatt, Hosington, and Butler

Original:

Take a chike, and draw him, and roste him, and lete the fete be on, and take awey the hede; then make batur of yolkes of eyron and floure, and caste ther-to pouder of ginger, and peper, saffron, and salt, and pouder hit faire til hit be rosted ynogh.

Ingredients:

1 roasting Chicken
2 egg yolks, beaten (Do not substitute a whole egg)
1 tsp flour
¼ tsp ginger
¼ tsp pepper
½ tsp salt
Optional: small pinch of saffron or yellow food coloring

Directions:

Roast the chicken, basting with the drippings to make the skin crispy.
About half an hour before it is done, brush it with the beaten egg yolk batter. Repeat the gilding once or twice until the chicken is done.

a Hen

❖ Viaunde of Cypres Ryalle (Chicken in Sweet Sauce)

Caellyn FitzHugh, Two Fifteenth-Century Cookery-Books, 1430-1450, England and France

This is an excellent cold chicken dish, suitable for lunches or any situation where you can prepare beforehand but have no reheating capability on the site. We hear from many new medieval cooks that this is one they get rave reviews on first time out. Caellyn's recipe is simplified from the one found in Cariadoc's *Miscelleny*; it is apparently intended for use with leftovers.

Serves 8-10 at a potluck or feast, 5-6 as a main dish.

Original:

Tak the braun of capounes or of hennes ysothe or rosted & bray it in a morter small as myed bred, & take good almound melk lyed with amoudyn or with floure of rys & colour it with safroun and boyle it wel. | & charge it with rosted brawn, and sesn with honey and salt, an florsche it with maces and quibybes.

Ingredients:

4 cups cooked chopped Chicken
1 cup white wine
¼ cup sugar
½ cup honey
½ tsp each ground cloves, mace, ginger
¼ cup ground almonds
½ cup currants (raisins will do in a pinch)

Directions:

Boil the wine and sugar together for 10 minutes or until it thickens and clings to the spoon. Add honey, spices, almonds, and raisins, and boil for another 5 minutes.

Arrange the cold cooked chicken in your serving dishes. Pour the hot syrup over the chicken. Chill well; serve cold.

Poultry & Rabbit

❖ Hotchpot de Poullaine (Chicken Casserole)

Siobhan Medhbh, le Viandier de Taillevent 1375-90, France
Serves 8-10 at a potluck or feast, 5-6 as a main dish.

Original:

Take your chicken, dismember it, and fry it lightly in lard. Take a bit of grilled bread and some chicken livers, steep in wine and beef broth, and boil with your meat. Grind ginger, cassia and grains of paradise, and steep in verjuice. It should be clearish black and not too thick.

Ingredients:

2 slices bread
4-5 lb roasting chicken, cut in pieces (keep the liver)
1 cup red wine
¾ cup beef broth
2 Tbsp butter or vegetable shortening
salt and pepper
2 Tbsp verjuice (see page 44)
2 tsp ground ginger
1 tsp ground cinnamon
¼ tsp. grains of paradise (seeds of 1 pod of cardamon crushed will substitute)

Directions:

Toast the bread, grind it fine, and soak in the wine and broth. Cut the chicken liver to fine pieces and process all of this in a food processor or blender. Reserve to use as a thickening.

Brown the chicken pieces in a heavy dutch oven or casserole. Add the breadcrumb mixture, salt, and pepper. Cover and simmer, either on top of the stove or in the oven (350 degrees) until the meat is just barely tender (about 30 minutes).

Stir the verjuice into the remaining spices and stir this mixture into the sauce in the pot. Cover, and continue cooking until the meat is falling off the bones. Take out the chicken and arrange nicely on a serving plate.

Boil the sauce until it is dark, glossy, and very thick. Spoon it over the chicken and serve.

Hotchpot de Poullaine (Chicken Casserole)   Traveling Dysshes

❖ Two Chikens from One (Stuffed Chicken)

Siobhan Medhbh, Pleyn Delit, 2nd edition, Heiatt, Hosington, and Butler, ISBN 0-8020-7632-7

This is one of my favorite of the medieval practical joke foods. They loved to make puns in food — and this dish, where you have one real and one faux chicken, is a great treat for feast and camping. If you're good at grill cooking or rotisserie, this is a good opportunity to show off at a camp sight.

Serves 8 at a feast.

Original:

Take your chicken, cut their throats, scald and pluck them, and makes sure that the skin is sound and whole. Do not refresh it in water. Take a pipe of straw or other material, insert it in between the skin and the flesh, inflate the skin, slit it between the shoulders without making too large a hole, and leave attached to the skin the thighs, feet, wings, and neck including the head.

To make the stuffing, take raw mutton, veal, pork, and pullet dark meat, chop them all together, and crush these in a mortar with some raw eggs, good harvest cheese, good Spice Powder, just a bit of saffron, and salt to taste. Fill your chicken and restitch the hole. From the rest of your stuffing make quenelles shapes like cake of woad. Cook them in beef broth and boiling water with plenty of saffron. Make sure they do not boil so vigorously that they fall apart. Spit your chickens and quenelles on a very thin iron spit. Glaze them with green or yellow. For the yellow glaze, take plenty of egg yolks, beat them well with a bit of saffron, and put the glaze on a plate or other dish. If you wish green glaze, crush greens with the eggs. After your chicken and quenelles are cooked, put the spit on the dish where the glaze is, throw the glaze all over, and put it back on the fire until the glaze sets. Do this two or three times. Make sure that the fire is not so big that the glaze burns.

Ingredients:

4-5 lb chicken
½ lb each lean chopped mutton, veal, pork and/or dark chicken meat
2 eggs, beaten
½ cup shredded fresh cheese (mozzarella, queso fresco, etc.) cheese
1 tsp Powder Forte (see recipe on page 38
1-2 threads saffron
salt and pepper to taste
1 cup beef broth
3-5 threads saffron
3 egg yolks, raw and beaten
5-8 threads saffron
1/4 cup chopped and crushed fresh parsley

Poultry & Rabbit   93

Directions:

Wash and pat dry the chicken. Remove the skin from the chicken by pulling up on the skin near one of the holes (neck or tail) and blowing air under the skin, between the flesh and the skin. Leave the wings and legs, including thighs, inside the skin, but remove the rest of the bird. Set aside. (If desired, soak the bird in a quart of water with 1 tsp salt added. Refrigerate.

Mix the meats, Powder Forte, 1-2 threads of saffron, and raw eggs to make a sausage-like concoction. Add Salt and Pepper to taste. Using the sausage, re-stuff the chicken skin until it looks like a chicken — the legs and wings will help. Stitch up the holes in neck and rump. From any leftover stuffing mix, make small quenelles (egg-shaped cakes) about the size of an extra-large egg.

Boil the beef broth and 3-5 threads saffron. Using a slotted spoon, gently lay the quenelles in the boiling liquid. Let them boil for a minute or two, or until they are brown on the outside. Remove them before they boil to pieces. Set aside for cooking later.

If you have a rotisserie, spit the both chickens — the faux one and the skinned one (and the quenelles, if you have a slender spit). Skewer the quenelles with bamboo or metal skewers and finish cooking them on the grill until they are lightly browned. Baste both chickens and the quenelles with the glaze two or three times during cooking. (For aesthetics, use only one color on each chicken.)

If you don't have a rotisserie, put the two chickens and the quenelles on a rack in a roasting pan. Roast at 350 for 45 minutes, then glaze as above. Return to the oven for 30 minutes, then glaze again. Test the internal temperature of the stuffing using a meat thermometer. When the stuffing reaches 165° F, glaze with any remaining glaze, return to the oven for 5 minutes, then serve out together on a nice platter.

Glazes

While the chickens are beginning to cook, make up the yellow and/or green glazes. For the green glaze, beat 3 egg yolks until glossy. Mix the parsley (including all juice that has come out from being crushed) with the eggs and set aside. Thin with ½ tsp. of water if necessary.. For the yellow glaze, beat 3 egg yolks until glossy. Crush the remaining saffron and mix well with the yolks.

Two Chikens from One (Stuffed Chicken)   Traveling Dysshes

❖ Conejas (Grilled Rabbit)

Siobhan Medbhdh, La Cocina, 1580, Spain

One really nice recipe, which would do very well at an outdoor event, is grilled rabbit. (You can substitute chicken if you like.)

Serves 8-10 at a potluck or feast, 5-6 as a main dish.

Original:

Take a plump rabbit and cut it in pieces. Take red wine and rosemary and sage, and canelle, and salt, and mayce, and mix them together with some oil; let the rabbit sit in it for 3 days before you want to serve it. Take the liquid and put it in a pot, stirring over the heat to make it thicker. Roast the meat over a hot fire, so the skin is crispy, brushing with the liquid. When it is done, serve it with aioli. [Translation from the Spanish by Pat McGregor, aka Siobhan Medhbh O'Roarke.]

Ingredients:

4 lb rabbit, cut up
3 cups red wine
2 Tbsp rosemary leaves
1 tsp sage, rubbed
2 tsp salt
½ tsp cinnamon
½ tsp mace
½ cup vegetable oil (olive oil is fine, but the flavor won't come through)

Directions:

Starting 72 hours before you serve, marinate the rabbit in the wine, spices, and oil. (I usually double bag this in freezer Ziplocs™.) Keep the bags in a bowl in the fridge (or once you leave for the site, in a cooler) and rotate and manipulate the bag once every 4-6 hours to make sure the marinade distributes evenly.

45 minutes before you're ready to eat, take the meat out of the marinade. Put the marinade juice in a pot and simmer until it's thickened slightly; use it to brush on the rabbit as it grills and as a table sauce. (Make sure it cooks at least 30 minutes.)

Grill the rabbit on an open fire or bed of charcoal, about 8 minutes per side (well done). Brush often with the sauce.

This works well as a rotisserie or spitted hare recipe, too.

The original recipe calls for an aioli (garlic mayonnaise) to go with the rabbit, which is incredibly good. (We watched Siobhan f. make a really

Poultry & Rabbit   95

scrumptious aioli in a mortar and pestle while camping at October crown –
which proves you really can do it!)

a Cook with Turnspits

Conejas (Grilled Rabbit)   Traveling Dysshes

❖ White Tharidah of Al-Rashid (Chicken Stew)

Sayyida Anahita al-Qurtubiyya bint 'abd al-Karim al-Fassi, Kitab al-Tabikh wa-islah al-Aghdiyah al-Ma'kulat by Abu Muhammad al-Muzaffar ibn Nasr ibn Sayyar al-Warraq, 10ᵗʰ Century,

Anahita says, "I usually cook this with Chicken. I have also cooked this as a vegetarian dish by doing one or more of the following: adding more chickpeas, tofu and/or seitan. You could try one of the commercial vegetarian chicken-substitutes (if you use Now & Zen's UnChicken, slice it before adding it to the pot, otherwise the flavors will not penetrate). You could also try adding unsweetened soy milk or almond milk"

Serves 8 at a potluck or feast, 4 as a main dish.

Original:

Take a chicken and joint it, or meat of a kid or lamb, and clean it and throw it in a pot, and throw on it soaked chickpeas, clean oil, galingale, cinnamon sticks, and a little salt. And when it boils, skim it. Take fresh milk and strain it over the pot and throw in onion slices and boiled carrots. And when it boils well, take peeled almonds and pound them fine. Break over them five eggs and mix with wine vinegar. Then throw in the pot and add coriander, a little pepper and a bit of cumin and arrange it and leave on the fire, and serve, God willing.

Ingredients:

1 chicken, cut up or parts equal in weight (about 5 lb) (cut chicken breast in half)
2 15-oz. cans chickpeas
3 Tbsp sesame oil (see note 1)
1 Tbsp galangal powder (see note 2)
6 cinnamon sticks (or 2 tsp ground cinnamon)
water as needed (or use liquid from canned chickpeas)
1 Tbsp salt, or to taste
1 cup whole milk (no kidding!)
1 large onion, quartered and sliced
1 lb carrots, cut up in circles or sticks
1 cup finely ground almonds
6 eggs
2 Tbsp red wine vinegar
1 Tbsp ground coriander seed
1 Tbsp ground cumin
1 tsp ground pepper, white or black
¼ cup finely chopped fresh coriander greens, aka cilantro (see note 3)

Directions:

In a large deep pot put chicken pieces, chickpeas with their liquid, oil, galangal, cinnamon, and salt. Add a minimal amount of water, if necessary. Bring to a boil, then turn down the heat and let simmer for 30 minutes, stirring to turn chicken pieces so they cook evenly.

Stir in milk, then add onion and carrots. Bring back to a slow simmer and cook 10 minutes. When chicken comes to a boil, reduce heat to medium and cook until onions and carrots are soft.

While chicken is cooking, in a medium sized bowl, crack the eggs and beat. Beat in the almonds and vinegar. Then stir in coriander, cumin and pepper and mix well.

After a few minutes, pour egg-almond mixture into the pot and stir. Lower heat and cook until eggs are set, a very few minutes.

Sprinkle with fresh torn coriander greens (optional). Traditionally this would probably have been served with a bread, something like a boulé. But it is also good with rice or couscous.

Notes

1. The oil most often called for in Middle Eastern recipes is sesame oil. This is NOT the roasted kind used in East Asian cooking. That would taste really wrong in this dish. Rather it is a light colored oil which you can find in health food stores and some Middle Eastern markets. If you can't find it, substitute olive oil.
2. Galangal (galaga alpinia) is a rhizome related to ginger used in Southeast Asian cooking, called Laos in Indonesian, lengkuas in Malay, and Kha in Thai. It tastes NOTHING like ginger. You should be able to find it at a spice merchant or an Asian market. Get powder or dried slices. If you use dried slices, just put 5 or 6 into the pot. You don't eat them, but they're nice to chew on. You could substitute 1 tsp ginger powder, but it doesn't taste the same.
3. Cilantro: if you really hate cilantro, substitute fresh Italian flat leaf parsley.

a Merchant Selling Spices

❖ A Recipe for a Dish of Chicken (or Partridge with Quince or Apple)

Anahita The Anonymous Andalusian cookbook, translated by Charles Perry, 13th Century, Andalusia

Anahita says, "The ingredients produce an interesting combination of flavors and textures. The breadcrumbs and eggs cook into a dumpling-like coating that you cut through as you serve, and which, because it has steamed over a very flavorful liquid, is quite tasty. I've never had the opportunity to use partridge. I have used either quince or apple, depending on availability. Quinces are usually available in the late fall and winter and make a very delightful dish. I have made this as a vegetarian dish, substituting tofu and/or seitan for the chicken (see above recipe on chicken substitutes)." Serves 8 at a potluck or feast, 4 as a main dish.

Original:

Leave overnight whichever of the two [birds] you have, its throat slit, in its feathers. Clean it and put it into a new pot and throw in two spoonfuls of rosewater and half a spoonful of good murri, two spoonfuls of oil, salt, a fennel stalk, a whole onion, and a quarter dirham of saffron, and water to cover the meat. Then take quince or apple, skin the outside and clean the inside and cut it up in appropriate-sized pieces, and throw them into the pot. Put it on a moderate fire and when it is done, take it away with a lid over it. Cover it with bread crumbs, a little sifted flour and five eggs, after removing some of the yolks. Cook it in the pot, and when the coating has cooked, sprinkle it with rosewater and leave it until the surface is clear and stands out apart. Ladle it out, sprinkle it with fine spices and present it.

Ingredients:

1 chicken cut up or parts equal in weight (about 5 lb) (cut chicken breast in half)
2 Tbsp rosewater (see note 4)
1 Tbsp murri (see note 5)
2 Tbsp oil (see note 1 above)
salt to taste (at least 2 tsp)
1 fennel bulb (also called *finocchio* in Italian markets)
1 onion, chopped
generous pinch saffron (see note 6)
water to cover
1 quince or apple, peeled, seeded and cut up in chunks (see note 7)
breadcrumbs from 5 slices white bread or challah, crusts removed
1/3 cup white flour
5 eggs
1 tsp rosewater
fine spices (see note 8)

Directions:

Clean the fowl and put it into a deep pot. I often leave the skin on as it makes a richer broth, but cut off the obvious fat. Add rosewater, murri, oil, salt, fennel stalk, onion, and saffron, and quince or apple. Then add water to cover the meat.

Bring to a boil, then reduce heat to and simmer. After it has been cooking about ½ hour, mix together breadcrumbs, eggs and flour in a bowl.

When the chicken is done, take it off the fire and spread it with breadcrumb mixture. Put back on the moderate fire, cover, and cook until the coating has set and is cooked through, about 10 minutes.

When the coating has cooked, sprinkle it with rosewater. Ladle out servings and sprinkle each dish with fine spices.

Notes

1. Different rosewaters are different strengths. I think the French kind one finds in the liquor aisle of the supermarket is stronger than the Lebanese kind I use (Cortas brand). Cortas was recommended to me as the best among several in both a Persian market and a Lebanese market. It is flavorful without being overwhelming. Test your rosewater to see how strong it is before you use it. Adjust the quantity if needed.

2. I was fortunate to be gifted with a jar of murri made by His Grace, Duke Cariadoc. However, I have made this dish without murri and didn't notice an appreciable difference in taste. So, if you don't have any murri, you can leave it out. If you would like to make your own murri, there are recipes on-line.

3. Saffron is an absolutely wonderful seasoning. Sure, it's expensive, but you usually only need a pinch. I highly recommend trying it out. Once you have it, be sure to keep it in an air and moisture tight container away from heat and light. If you don't have any, omit it. The dish will certainly lack the flavor and fragrance, but there is no substitute.

4. Quinces are really fragrant and when cooked are delicious. So if you can find one, I highly recommend you use it rather than an apple.

5. This is not the same as European poudre forte or fine spice powder. I have not found a recipe, so I use a combination of spices commonly used together in this source. ½ tsp ground coriander seed, ¼ tsp ground cumin, ¼ tsp ground pepper, ½ tsp pounded lavender buds (optional), 1/8 tsp ground cinnamon (either Ceylon cinnamon or the more common cassia - the so-called cinnamon one finds in the supermarket. They taste rather different. Use whichever you prefer). You can alter the amounts you use based on what is available and your personal taste.

Meat

For most nobles in period, meat was a major dish, especially in the depths of winter when vegetables and fruit laid by were getting thin in the bottom of the barrel. When most of us think of "Medieval Feasts," we see Henry with that turkey leg in his fist. In period, meat was most often served stewed, chopped, or ground, to help spread the available nutrition around as well as to deal with tough, gamey flesh. So, in this section, our recipes have an even measure of roasts and other ways to prepare meat.

❖ Yrchouns (Sausage Hedgehogs)

Siobhan Medhbh, Two Fifteenth-Century Cookery-Books, Harleian MS. 279, 1430, England and France

This is a wonderful illusion food, so beloved of the medievals, and it tastes good too! Serve on a bed of greens or parsley. One way to spiff up a head table entry or potluck presentation is to make one large "mama" hedgehog and surround her with her babies. The original recipe calls for sausage in casings, colored with various "endorings" at the end. The recipe as it is redacted here is in the "traditional" SCA manner. Most SCA beginning cooks are not eager to work with sausage casings, and some feast-goers will avoid them.

You can substitute commercial sausage here; if so, use the sage flavored sausage for a more interesting and unusual flavor. You may wish to add in ginger anyway. Serves 6-8 at a potluck or feast, 3-4 as a main dish. (This dish is *very* popular, we think because it's cute *and* familiarly flavored.)

Original:

Take Piggis mawy & skalde hem wel; take groundyn Porke & knede it with Spicerye, with Pouder Gyngere, and Salt and Sugre; do it on the mawe, but fill it nowt to fulle, then sew hem with a fayre threde and putte hem in a Spete as men don piggys. Take blaunchid Almoundys and kerf hem long, smal, and scharpe, & frye hem in grece and sugre. Take a litel pryke and prycjje the yrchouns. An putte in the hole the Almundys, every hole half, & leche fro other. Ley hem then to the fyre, when they are rostid, dore hem, sum with Whete of Flowre and mylke of Almaundys, some grene, sume blacke with Blode, and lat hem nowt browne to moche; & serve forth.

Meat

Ingredients:

1 lb each ground pork and lamb
1 tsp each ginger and sage
½ tsp mace
1 tsp salt
2 ½ oz blanched and slivered almonds
tiny black currants or capers (optional)

Directions:

Mix the meat and spices (not the nuts), and set aside overnight for the spices to blend. (If you don't have time, that's OK, but the meat will be less strongly flavored.)

Form into egg-shaped and egg-sized balls with pointed ends, flattened slightly on the bottom. Place in a baking pan – these have a tendency to give off grease, so make sure it's a pan that will catch the drips. Push the slivered almonds into the back of the hedgehogs, pointing in one direction like the quills on the animal's back. Use 8-10 spines per hedgehog to give the proper effect.

[If you are interested in handling sausage casings, make your hedgehogs about 3" long, tied off between with thread or two (2) knots in the casing. You can cut them apart after cooking or before, but it is easier to handle them if you cut them before cooking.]

Bake covered at 350 degrees F. for about 30 minutes, or until medium brown. Drain on brown paper bags for a minute or two before arranging and serving. Serve hot. (Lady Ilsa von Thuringen of Crosston uses currants as tiny eyes, added on after the beasties are baked but before you serve them. Siobhan has begun using capers for this purpose.)

a Woman Milking a Cow

Yrchouns (Sausage Hedgehogs)   Traveling Dysshes

❖ Stewed Beeff (Braised/Stewed Beef)

Siobhan Medhbh, Two Fifteenth-Century Cookery-Books, 1430-1450, England and France

This recipe does not explicitly call for the breadcrumbs as a thickening, but it does call for a "sirippe" of the juice from the cooking. Most syrups are thickened; hence the use of breadcrumbs to thicken the sauce. Serves 10 at a potluck or feast, 5 as a main dish.

Original:

Take faire Ribbes of ffresh beef, and (if thou wilt) roste hit til hit be nyghe ynowe, then put hit in a faire possenet; cast therto parcely and onyons mynced, reysons of couraunes, powder peper, canel, cloves, saundres, safferon, and salt; then caste there-to wyn and a littul vynegre; sette a lyd on the potte, and lete hit boile sokingly on a faire charcole til hit be ynogh, then lay the fflessh, in disshes and the sirippe there-vppon, And serve it forth.

Ingredients:

2-3 lb beef, cut in cubes for stewing (you may use boneless stew beef if you
    will)
½ cup flour
5 Tbsp oil
5-6 cups beef stock
2 tsp salt
½ tsp each: cinnamon, cloves, mace
1 tsp saunders (sandalwood)
¼ cup raisins or currants
4 black peppercorns
¼ cup wine (whatever you have handy)
¼ cup vinegar
pinch saffron

Directions:

Coat the meat in the flour; brown in oil. Add the stock, spices and herbs except for the saffron. Simmer for 2 hours.

While the stew is cooking, let the crumbs soak in the vinegar and saffron. Mix together well (or run through a mortar and pestle or food processor). Stir the bread mixture into the stew; let simmer 5-10 minutes to thicken. Check the seasoning (especially the salt); season to taste, serve.

This goes particularly well with barley dishes, noodles, stewed turnips, and the like.

Meat   103

❖ Bor in Counfett (Ham Slices in Honey Glaze)

Kay of Triastrium, Ancient Cookery

Another excellent way to serve a common meat in a new guise. For most of us, though, the extra decoration on the plate is a bit beyond our pocketbooks. Serves 8 at a potluck or feast, 4 as a main dish.

Original:

Take felittes of braun and let hem lye in a merlous and houre, and then parboyle hem, and roile hem, and do in a pot clarifiet honey and wyn togethere, and put therto pouder of peper, and of cloves, and there hit that it be thyk, and in the thykennynge bounden to the fellettes, then take hem out of the pot, and lay hem as a bourdre to kele, and whan thei ben cooled dresse them for the shew in a dysshe, and beside hem some barses of silver, and in the mydward a barre of golde, and serue it forth.

Ingredients:

1 lb ham, cut in thick (1/2") slices
½ cup honey
½ cup white wine
¼ tsp ground cloves
pinch pepper

Directions:

Cook wine, honey, and spices over medium heat until thickened. Dredge the ham slices in the sauce, arrange on a plate, and cool. Serve cold.

a Cowherd with His Cows

Bor in Counfett (Ham Slices in Honey Glaze)   Traveling Dysshes

❖ For to make Alawder de beef (Stuffed Beef Rolls)

Siobhan Medhbh, A noble boke of festes ryalle and Cokery (1500).

These are fun, easy, and great on a camping trip, as they can be cooked in a pan, on a spit, on skewers, or directly on a grate. Makes 4 "beef birds."

Original

To make Alawder de beef take the clodde of beef and make leches of a span longe / than take percely and hewe it smale with shepe talowe & take pouder of peper & canelle and medle it al togyder & cast therto salte & couche one leche with rawe yolkes of egges & rolle vp the leche and prycke theym close & put theym on a smale broche & rolle them vp and serue them in a gode syrupe.

And, from the Beinecke Manuscript "MS Beinecke 163"

"Take lyr of beef; cut hem in lechys. Lay hem abrode on a bord. Take the fatte of motyn, or of beef, herbys & onions hewyn togefyr, & strew hit on the leches of beef with poudyr of pepyr & a lytyl salt, & roll hit up therynne. Put hem on a broch; rost hem."

Ingredients:

4 "minute" steaks (or 4 steaks cut ¼" thick, about ¼ lb. each)
1 tsp. minced fresh parsley (or ¼ tsp. of dried parsley leaves, crumbled)
1 small onion, finely minced
3 boiled eggs yolks, crumbled
1 tsp. lard, bone marrow, butter, or other shortening
¼ tsp ginger
¼ tsp. salt
several threads of saffron)
¼ C cider vinegar, or verjuice
pinch of ginger, pepper

Directions

In a small bowl, mix together onion, egg yolks, parsley, fat, ginger, salt, and saffron. This should make a spread the consistency of crunchy peanut butter. If it needs more liquid, add a few drops of vinegar. Spread this mixture on the steaks, then roll them up. Secure them with bamboo skewers (or, alternately, toothpicks or string). Broil for about 10-15 minutes, just turning to brown all the way around

While they are cooking, mix together the vinegar and remaining spices.

When they are nicely browned, put them on a serving dish. Sprinkle your sauce over them, and serve out.

Alternately, thin slices of lamb or pork will work.

Meat

❖ Bourbelier of Fresh Boar (Roast Pork)

Siobhan Medhbh, Le Menagier, 1393, Paris.
This is a lovely roast for a feast, and serves up well. Serves 16.

Original:

First you must put it in boiling water, and take it out quickly and stick it with cloves; put it on to roast, and baste with a sauce made of spices, that is ginger, cinnamon, clove, grain, long pepper and nutmegs, mixed with verjuice, wine, and vinegar, and without boiling use it to baste; and when it is roasted, it should be boiled up together. And this sauce is called boar's tail, and you will find it later (and there it is thickened with bread: and here, not)

Ingredients:

3 lb pork roast, boneless
50-60 whole cloves
½ tsp grains of paradise
¼ tsp ginger
1/8 tsp cinnamon
1 tsp pepper, coarse ground
¼ tsp nutmeg
½ cup verjuice (or sour apple juice)
¾ cup wine
¾ cup vinegar

Directions:

Preheat oven to 450 degrees F. Stud roast with whole cloves, baste with a mixture of the remaining ingredients, then put into oven. Immediately after putting it in, turn oven down to 350 degrees F. Roast meat 1 hour 45 minutes (for this size roast), basting every 15 minutes. [If you hate basting as much as I do, you can pour all the sauce over the roast, seal the roast in a clay pot or with foil, and keep it covered until done.]

another Pig

❖ Braun en Peurade (Pork in Pepper Sauce)

Gwyneth Felton and Serena Holmes, Two Fifteenth-Century Cookery-Books, 1430-1450, England and France

Note that this recipe calls for Saunders, which is a ground sandalwood spice. While the stew is delightful without it, it takes on a real period flair (and is really yummy) with the saunders, and there really isn't an adequate substitute (waving your sandalwood fan over it isn't going to help). You can get saunders from the Pepperer's Guild, listed on page 30

Original:

Take wyn, pouder of Canell, draw hit through a Streynour, set hit ouer the fire, lete hit boile, caste there-to maces cloues, powder of Peper; take smale onyons hole, parboyle hem, caste there-to; let hem boile togider; then take Brawne, leche hit, but not to thin; And if hit be saused, let stepe hit in Hote water til hit be tender, then cast hit into the siripe; take Saundres, Vynegar, and caste there-to, and lete boile al togidre til hit be ynowe; then take pouder of ginger, caste theto; let hit not be thik ne to thyn, butte as potage shulde be; and Serue hit forthe.

Ingredients:

2 lb boneless pork diced into 1" cubes
5 oz smoked ham, diced into 1" cubes
½ cup flour
2 Tbsp butter
4 cups chicken broth (lightly salted)
2 cups red wine
12 small white onions
1-2 tsp salt
2 tsp saunders
1 tsp cinnamon
1/3 tsp whole cloves
1 tsp mace, ground or grated
1 tsp pepper
1 cup finely crushed breadcrumbs
2 Tbsp vinegar

Directions:

Dredge the pork and ham in flour; brown in butter. Add the broth, wine, onions, saunders, and spices, and simmer for about 2 hours, or until the onions are soft. Take out the onions, crush them with the back of a spoon (or puree in a food processor). Put the onions back in the pot and simmer for another half hour.

Meat 107

While the stew is simmering, let the breadcrumbs soak in the vinegar. Mash well (or puree in a blender or processor), and at the end of the simmering time add it to the stew. Cook for 10-15 minutes more to thicken.

Serve (works wonderfully in hollowed out bread rounds). This stew freezes extremely well.

a Man Braying Spices in a Pestle

Braun en Peurade (Pork in Pepper Sauce)   Traveling Dysshes

❖ Civé de Veel (Veal Stew)

Siobhan Medhbh, le Viandier de Taillevent 1375-90, France

Taillevent gives two possible thickenings, but Siobhan finds the breadcrumbs work most dependably for her. Serves 8 at a potluck or feast, 5 as a main dish.

Original:

Roast it on the spit or grill without letting it cook too much, cut it into pieces, and fry it lightly in lard with onions cut very small. Take grilled bread steeped in wine and beef broth or puree of peas, and boil with your meat. Grind ginger, cassia, cloves, grains of paradise, and saffron (to give it color), and steep in verjuice and vinegar. There should be enough onions; the bread should be browned; and it should be thick, sour with vinegar, spicy and golden.

Ingredients:

2 – 2 1/2 lb boneless veal
2 Tbsp lard, solid vegetable shortening, or oil
5 medium onions, chopped fine
2 tsp ground ginger
2 tsp ground cinnamon
1/2 tsp ground cloves
seeds from one cardamom pod
pinch saffron
salt and pepper
2-3 tsp verjuice (see page 44)
2-3 tsp vinegar
4 cups chicken broth (lightly salted)

Directions:

Cut veal in 1" cubes. In a casserole, heat the shortening or lard and fry half the veal until brown on all sides. Remove; brown the remaining half. Remove and set aside.

Add the onions and cook until soft and transparent (not brown!). Add 3 cups of broth, and return the meat to the pot. Slowly stir the thickening mixture (see below) into it, and cover the pot.

Mix the ginger, cinnamon, cloves, cardamom, and saffron. If your spices are freshly ground, you may want to grind the mix together in a mortar and pestle.

Bring the stew to a boil. Stir in a quarter cup of the juice from the pot into the mixture of spices (except salt and pepper), and then stir the resulting mixture back into the stew. Add salt and pepper to taste, cover and simmer until the meat falls apart (1 - 1.5 hours). Stir in the vinegar and verjuice, more or less depending on taste.

This freezes really well, and is something that can be made in advance for events, potlucks, or camping.

Thickening 1:
4 slices of bread
¾ cup red or white wine
1 cup beef stock, strained

Heat the oven to 350 degrees F.; bake the bread for 3 minutes or until golden brown on both sides. Let cool and grind fine (either with food processor or by mashing in a resealable plastic bag with a rolling pin). Stir in the wine, let stand 5 minutes, then add the beef broth.

Thickening 2:
1/4 cup dried split green peas, soaked overnight and drained
1 1/2 cup water
salt and pepper

Simmer the peas covered, in water until very soft (1 ½ – 2 hours). Mash in a food processor, mortar and pestle, or vegetable mill. The puree should be thick but still pour easily. Season to taste with salt and pepper.

a Heifer

Civé de Veel (Veal Stew)　　　　　　　　　　Traveling Dysshes

❖ Mortrews Blank (Chicken & Pork Hash)

Cordelia Toser, Forme of Cury, 1390, England and France

This dish is typical of those meant for invalids, but is surprisingly tasty. The previous recipe states that the meats are to be stewed, then cut into small pieces and ground "to dust". Serve it to 4-6, surrounded by toasted triangles of bread.

Original:

Take pork and hennes and seeth hem as to fore. Bray almaundes blaunched, and temper hem vp with the self broth, and alye the fleissh with the mylke and white flour of rys; and boile it, & do therin powdour of gynger, sugur and salt, and look that it be stondyng.

Ingredients:

¾ lb boneless pork roast
1 ¼ lb chicken thighs & legs
water to cover meats
1/3 cup whole almonds
        2-3 cups broth (saved from initial cooking of meats)
1 Tbsp rice flour
1 ½ each tsp ginger, sugar
2 tsp salt

Directions:

In a 3-quart saucepan, place cut up chicken pieces and coarsely chopped pork. Cover with water and cook on moderate heat for 45 minutes. Remove from heat. Discard chicken bones and skin. Chop the meat. Save broth for making almond milk.

In a small saucepan, blanch almonds for 10 minutes, cool. Remove skins and puree almonds in a blender with 1 cup broth until almond pieces are small. Pour off the resulting milky liquid and strain it. Put more broth with the same almonds and puree again. Pour off resulting liquid and strain. Continue until 1 cup almond milk is produced.

Place rice flour in large saucepan, stir in small amount of almond milk until smooth, then add remaining almond milk. Cook on high heat until thickened – about 10 minutes. Stir in seasonings. Chop meat in small batches in blender, then add to almond mixture. Cook on medium heat, stirring occasionally, until thickened – about 40 minutes. Correct seasoning to taste.

Meat   111

❖ Stekys of Venson or Bef (Venison or Beef Steaks)

Kay of Triastrium, Pleyn Delit, A Fifteenth Century Coke Book, England and France

Here's a great dish when confronted by folks who are rapacious carnivores, and who claim never to have seen enough meat on a feast table! Serves 6 folk of moderate appetite.

Original:

To make Stekys of venson or bef. Take Venyson or Bef & leche & gredyl it up brown; then take Vynegre & a litel verious <verjuice>, & a lytil Wyne, and putte pouder perpir ther-on y-now and pouder Gyngere; and atte the dressoure straw on pouder Canelle y-now, that the stekys be all y-helid ther-wyth, and but a litel sauce; & serve it forth.

Ingredients:

6 fairly thin beef steaks
oil or fat for grilling
¼ cup vinegar
2 Tbsp verjuice (see p 44)
4 Tbsp red wine
pinch each of ground black pepper and ginger
½ tsp cinnamon

Directions:

Make the sauce and set it aside to steep the flavors together.

Rinse your steaks, and, if desired, slice the fat on the edges to prevent curling. Pat dry. Broil or grill on a griddle. When the steak is cooked to your liking (rare, medium, well-done), take it off the fire and spread the sauce over it, and serve it forth.

Sauce:

Mix the liquids and spices together. Whisk or beat until it is all smooth.

Balsalmic vinegar would be splendid in this recipe. We have records dating it back to the eleventh century. A Benedictine monk called Donizone recorded the gift of a barrel of vinegar given as a present by Marquess Bonifacio, lord of Canossa and Empress Matilda's father, to the King and future Emperor Enrico II of Franconia in 1046. This cask of vinegar had a distinctive sweet and sour taste, and a dark color.

Stekys of Venson or Bef (Venison or Beef Steaks)   Traveling Dysshes

❖ Poumes (Meatball Apples)

Cordelia Toser, Two Fifteenth-Century Cookery-Books, Harleian Ms. 279, 1430, England and France

Many recipes for poumes produce a soft white meatball, but Cordelia prefers a firmer texture and so bakes them instead of boiling. The yellow-green coating turns them into a subtlety. Serves 4-6.

Original:

Take fayre buttys of Vele & hew hem, and grynd hem in a morter, & wyth the zolkys of eyroun, with the whyte of eyroun; an caste ther-to powder Pepyr, Canel, Gyngere, Clowys powther, & datys y-mynced, Safroun, & raysonys of Coraunce, an sethe in a panne wyth fayre water, an let it boyle; than wete thin handys in Raw eyroun, than take it an rolle it in thin honeys, smaller or gretter, as thow wolt haue it, an caste it in-to boyling water, an let boyle y-now; than putte it on a Spete round, and lete hem rosty; then take flowre an zolkys of eyroun, an the whyte, an draw hem thorwe a straynowre, an caste ther-to pouder Gyngere, an make thin bature grene with the Ius of Percely, of Malwys, in tyme of zere Whete, and caste on the pommys as they turne a-boute, & serue forth.

Ingredients:

Meatballs:
1 cup chopped dates
1 cup raisins
½ tsp salt
1/8 tsp pepper
½ tsp cinnamon
¼ tsp each ginger, cloves
    1 lb ground veal or pork
2 eggs, beaten
1/8 tsp ground saffron

Batter:
½ cup flour
1 egg yolk
¼ tsp ginger
1/ 8 tsp ground saffron
    3 Tbsp fresh chopped parsley or 1 Tbsp parsley juice
12 toothpicks
12 fresh mint leaves

Meat 113

Directions:

   Lightly grease baking pan. Preheat oven to 375 degrees F.
   Mix fruits, spices and beaten eggs together. Thoroughly mix in meat. Wet fingers in ice water, form 12 apple-shaped balls from the meat mixture and place them on the cooking pan. Cook for 20 minutes, then cool to room temperature.
   Mix flour, egg yolk, spices and parsley together. Use pastry brush to coat "apples" with batter and place them on fresh baking pan. Cook only until golden, not browned – about 6-7 minutes.
   Insert a toothpick "stem" in each apple so that it pierces one end of the mint leaf and arrange the "apples" on a serving dish.

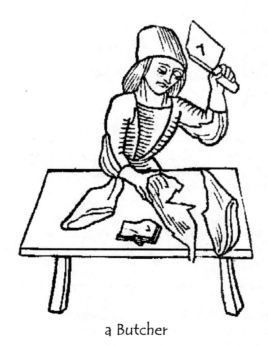

a Butcher

Poumes (Meatball Apples)   Traveling Dysshes

Soups

"Soup of the Evening, Beautiful Soup!" Soup is another of those ubiquitous dishes — how else do we use leftovers so thriftily, make palatable tough meat or fowl that can't be served roasted or grilled, and warm the hearts of our friends and neighbors on a cold night.

❖ Roo Broth (Venison Soup)

Siobhan Medhbh, Forme of Cury, 1390, England and France
This is an excellent way to use up leftovers of venison, or, if you are lacking that particular meat, beef or pork. The soup freezes well and travels well.
Serves 8-10 at a potluck or feast, 5-6 as a main dish.

Original:

Roo broth wel to the same seruyse. Take venysoun & wasch it and culpoun it in a fyngerbroede & perboyle it; & than tak it yp & streyne the broth & do water to the venysoun, & pike it clene, & put it into the broth. & sette it ouer the feere, & do therto salt and percely and ysope and suerey and poudere of peper ,and late sethe til it be tendre; & do therto poudre of coloure & of maces & canel and | quibibes, but look it be nought to hot.

Ingredients:

1 lb boneless venison, cooked and cut into small pieces
1 ½ cups each water and red wine
¾ cup breadcrumbs (the darker the bread, the better)
½ cup vinegar (preferably red wine or Balsamic)
¼ tsp each ginger, cinnamon, mace
1 tsp salt
½ cup currants or raisins
½ cup blood or 1 tsp Marmite or other gravy coloring

Directions:

Cover the chopped venison with wine and water; simmer for about an hour,
While the meat is simmering, soak the breadcrumbs in vinegar.
Mix together the spices, currants, and blood/Marmite. Stir into the soup, and let simmer for 30-45 minutes more, or until the venison is extremely tender.
Mix the breadcrumbs and vinegar into the broth, stirring well over medium high heat until the mixture thickens. Serve at once.

Soups

❖ Sowpys Dorre (Onions on Toast)

Siobhan Medhbh, Forme of Cury, 1390, England and France

"Sowpys" were slices of toast: all recipes for "soppes" or "sowpys" therefore include toast with some sort of broth or juice over it. With vegetarian broth this is a vegetarian soup.

Serves 8-10 at a potluck or feast, 4 as a main dish.

Original:

Nym onyons and mynce hem smale & frye hem in oyle dolyf. Nym wyn & boyle yt with the onyouns. Toste wyte bred & do yt in dischis, & god almande mylk also, & do the wyne with onyons aboue & serve yt forth.

Ingredients:

½ cup olive oil
4 large white onions, sliced into rings
salt and fresh ground pepper
1 cup heavy cream
¼ tsp nutmeg
4 slices of white or whole wheat toast, cut in strips or triangles.

Directions:

Heat the oil in a deep skillet and add the onions. Sauté over low heat, stirring frequently, until the onions are soft and nearly transparent. Add salt and pepper to taste. Take the pot off the heat, stir the cream and nutmeg in gently. Return to low heat, but do not allow the mixture to boil (else the cream will curdle).

Arrange the toast on plates; when the soppes is heated through, pour over the toast and serve.

You can also add vegetarian or chicken broth and serve as a soup.

a Stag Couchant

❖ Green Broth of Eggs & Cheese Soup (Green Egg & Cheese Soup))

Siobhan Medhbh, Le Menagier, 1393, Paris.
Dr. Seuss fans will be thrilled to see that there really are Green Eggs! These are really yummy, in either the vegetarian or carnivore version. Serves 4.

Original:

Take parsley and a little cheese and sage and a very small amount of saffron, moistened bread, and mix with water left from cooking peas, or stock, grind and strain: And have ground ginger mixed with wine, and put on to boil; then add cheese and eggs poached in water, and let it be a bright green. Item, some do not add bread, but instead of bread use bacon.

Ingredients:

1/8 cup breadcrumbs (commercial; if you use your own bread, use two slices of white bread)
2 1/2 cups pea stock or chicken stock (I thin it some with fresh water)
A medium bunch of fresh parsley, or 2 Tbsp dried parsley
2-3 fresh sage leaves (1/16 oz, approximately)
pinch saffron
2 oz cheese, finely grated
1/4 tsp ground ginger (fresh), or 1/8 tsp dried ginger powder
2 Tbsp white wine
2 more oz finely grated cheese
4 eggs
1/8 cup breadcrumbs

Directions:

First, soak the breadcrumbs in the stock. Grind parsley, sage, and saffron in a mortar thoroughly; add ½ oz cheese and soaked bread and grind together. Strain through a strainer; if necessary, put back in mortar what didn't go through, grind again, and strain again. (You can use a food processor if you don't have a mortar. Make a fine slurry.)

Mix wine and ginger, add to mixture, and heat over medium flame until it begins to boil. Stir carefully — this can stick very easily.

Stir in the rest of the cheese until it melts. With one hand, stir the pot briskly. Break each egg into the mixture, stirring while the eggs form into wispy threads. (Alternately, you can poach the eggs in a separate pot and add to the mixture once the cheese has melted. This requires more careful handling with the eggs as you transfer them.) Serve immediately.

❖ Jowtes of Almand Mylke (Green Almond Soup)

Cordelia Toser, Pleyn Delit
Serves 8 at a potluck or feast, 4 as a main dish.

Original:

Take erbes; boile hem, hewe hem, and grynde hem smale; and drawe hem up with water. Set hem on the fire and seeth the jowtes with the mylke; and cast theron sugar & salt, and serue it forth.

Ingredients:

10 oz chopped blanched spinach
3-4 spring onions, cut into pieces
3 sprigs fresh parsley
1 ¼ cup ground almonds
1 ½ tsp salt
1 tsp sugar
6 cups water

Directions:

Grind almonds, onions and parsley together in a blender until almonds resemble corn meal. Put spinach, salt, sugar and water into stockpot. Add almond mixture and cook on medium heat 10-15 minutes. Serve hot or cold.

a Man Warming His Feet

❖ Salomene (Fish Soup)

Cordelia Toser, Take a Thousand Eggs, Vol. 2

The spices sprinkled on at the end make the difference between a blah and a tasty soup. I suggest you only use flower petals that are organically grown.

Serves 6-8 at a potluck or feast, 4 as a main dish.

Original:

Take gode Wyne, and gode pouder, & Brede y-ground, an sugre, an boyle it y-fere; than take Trowtys, Rochys, Perchys, other Carpys, other alle these y-fere, and make hem clene, & aftere roste hem on a Grydelle; than hewe hem in gobettys: whan they ben y-sothe, fry hem in oyle a lytil, then caste in the brwet; and whan thou dressist it, take Maces, Clowes, Quybibes, Gelofrys; and cast a-boue, & serue forth.

Ingredients:

2/3 cup sweet white wine
1 1/3 cup water
¼ cup breadcrumbs
½ tsp sugar
¼ tsp ginger
2/3 lb trout or perch, skinned, boned, and cut into bite-sized pieces
3 Tbsp olive oil
1 tsp each powdered cubebs, cloves, mace
fresh flower petals (optional)

Directions:

Mix water, wine, breadcrumbs, sugar and ginger in stockpot and cook gently for 5-10 minutes.

Saute fish in oil in skillet until fish turns opaque. Add drained fish to stockpot and cook gently about 10 more minutes or until fish is done.

Sprinkle powdered spices and flower petals over each serving.

Soups 119

a Seller of Goats' Milk

Salomene (Fish Soup)   Traveling Dysshes

Beverages

Most of the time, if you have a Western European persona and want to be completely authentic, you will want to serve your guests beer, wine, or mead. You can also serve chilled fruit juice, and in later periods (especially after 1450), shaved ice with juice over it. Lemonade and cherry ade are generally well-liked.

Expecially out where we are camping, it's important to keep plenty of fluids on hand. If you keep carboys of water on hand, particularly in a crockery dispenser or a "bubbler" with a cloth cover, you can provide drinks without disrupting the ambiance too severely.

Sekanjabin, below, is a good cooling drink with lots of good replenishing electrolytes. We particularly like it in hot weather, but Cariadoc and his family drink it year round.

❖ Sekanjabin (Oxymel)

Cariadoc and Elizabeth, Andalusian

This is the only recipe in the Miscelleny that is based on a modern source: *A Book of Middle Eastern Food* by Claudia Roden. Sekanjabin is a period drink; it is mentioned in the Fihrist of al-Nadim, which was written in the tenth century AD. The only period recipe I have found for it (in the Andalusian cookbook) is called Sekanjabin Simple and omits the mint. It is one of a large variety of similar drinks described in that cookbook – flavored syrups intended to be diluted in either hot or cold water before drinking.

This seems to be at least two different recipes, for two different medical uses. The first, at least, is intended to be drunk hot. In modern Iranian restaurants sekanjabin is normally served cold, often with grated cucumber.

Original:

Take a ratl of strong vinegar and mix it with two ratls of sugar, and cook all this until it takes the form of a syrup. Drink an ŭqiya of this with three of hot water when fasting: it is beneficial for fevers of jaundice, and calms jaundice and cuts the thirst, since sekanjabin syrup is beneficial in phlegmatic fevers: make it with six ŭqiyas of sour vinegar for a ratl of honey and it is admirable.

Beverages

Ingredients:

4 cups sugar
2 ½ cups water
1 cup wine vinegar
handful mint leaves, chopped

Directions:

Dissolve sugar in water; when it comes to a boil add vinegar. Simmer ½ hour. Add mint, remove from heat, let cool. Dilute the resulting syrup to taste with ice water (5 to 10 parts water to 1 part syrup). The syrup stores without refrigeration.

an Ale Seller

Sekanjabin (Oxymel)   Traveling Dysshes

❖ Cordials

Flavoring alcoholic beverages goes back at least to Pliny the Elder in 77 A.D., although they generally were making a medicinal drink until late in our period. Cordelia has not tried making Pliny's Turnip Wine made from turnip juice and grape must, which surely fits into the medicinal category.

As early as the end of the 14th century, distilled spirits (aquimirabelis, aqua vitae or aqua ardaunt) or brandies were sometimes added to flavored wines. By the early 1600's it is clearly evident that alcoholic beverages were sometimes drunk for pleasure. Wine was flavored with cherries, lemons, currants, walnuts, or flower petals; cinnamon or other spices were sometimes added.

What Cordelia makes is a combination of several recipes.

❖ To Make The Surfit Water (Dried Fruit Cordial)

Cordelia Toser, Martha Washington's Booke of Cookery #288, 1550-1625
Original:
Take a peck of poppy flowers, clip them & cut the blacks clean out, & steep them in 3 quarts of Aquavity, then strayne out your poppies & put in 2 quarts of the best sack, 4 ounces of raysons of the sun stoned, as much figgs slyced, 2 ounces of licorish slyced, 20 cloves, 20 cornes of whole pepper. let all these be put into a bottle & sweetned with sugar. put in 2 ounces of annyseeds bruised,& soe let them stand for a moneth, then strayne it, & bottle it up in glasses, & corke it close, & soe keep it for your use.

Ingredients:

8 ounces dried cherries
4–6 whole black peppercorns
½ stick cinnamon
1 cup sweet white wine (Cordelia uses white Zinfandel)
1 ½ cups vodka
½ cup sugar

Directions:

Place all ingredients in a quart glass jar with a tight-fitting lid. Stir the contents daily by shaking the jar, and keep the jar away from heat sources such as direct sunlight.

After two weeks the sugar should have dissolved completely. At that time you may discard the drained fruit or save it to use as a dessert topping.

Filter the liquid so that it is clear – sediment or cloudy stuff is unattractive to our modern eyes. Then put your cordial in an attractive bottle and serve. This is not a long-lived beverage and should be drunk with 6 months of bottling.

❖ To Make Raspberry Wine (Fresh Fruit Cordial)

Cordelia Toser, The Queen's Closet Opened, 1655

If you don't care for raspberries, make cordial from strawberries, blackberries, peaches, apricots, plums, orange peel, lemon peel, rose petals, walnuts or blanched almonds. The pits from peaches and apricots should not be used for health reasons.

Original:

Take a gallon of good Rhenish Wine, put into it as much Rasberries very ripe as will make it strong, put it in an earthen pot, and let it stand two days; then pour your Wine from the Rasberries, and put into every bottle two ounces of sugar. Stop it up and keep it by you.

Ingredients:

6 baskets fresh raspberries
½ gallon moderately priced vodka
2 or more cups sugar

Directions:

Place the washed raspberries in a 5 liter glass jar with a lid. Pour the vodka over the berries until they are submerged. Put the jar lid on loosely, so that dust and insects cannot get in, but any fermentation gasses can dissipate harmlessly. After a month to 6 weeks remove the fruit.

Filter the liquid into a smaller jar; then put the jar away for 3 to 6 months to age. At this point fasten the lid on tightly, as there should be no fermentation at this stage. You want the jar full to minimize the amount of air touching your liquid. At the end of the aging process (the contents will smell more like raspberries than medicinal alcohol by then), stir in 1 cup sugar.

After that dissolves (about 10 minutes), stir in another cup of sugar, then taste the liquid to see if it needs more sugar. It probably will.

When you get it sweet enough to your taste, bottle the cordial, get out your small glasses and enjoy. If you drink slowly, as Cordelia does, refrigerate the finished cordial, but in any case expect to drink it within a year of bottling.

Desserts

Who doesn't love desserts? It's nice to have a sweet at the end of the meal, and it's nice to have something else to make other than shortbread. In Elizabethan times, at some events there would be a dessert table after the main meal, where desserts, beverages, cheese and fruit would be available for those who wanted to browse on the goodies while chatting or visiting. It's an exceptional way to provide for bardics, dancing events, and other events where formal seating may be adverse to good conversation and fun.

❖ Wardonys in Syryp (Pears in Wine Syrup)

Gwyneth Felton and Serena Holmes, Two Fifteenth-Century Cookery-Books, Harleian 279.10, 1430, England and France

These pears in syrup are an excellent way to end a meal. They grace a dessert table, although you must remember to include eating implements for your diners.

Do not use Bartlett pears, as they are too soft to stand up to the cooking involved. Check with your local market for a fresh, tart pear that is firmer.

The fastest way to make this dessert is to use canned half pears; the resulting dish will be less strongly flavored, but if you are in a hurry or doubt your ability to cook the fresh pears, it is an option. Use the ones packed in water or juice rather than in heavy syrup.

Serves 8 at a potluck, 4 at home.

Original:

Take Wardonys, and caste on a potte, and boyle hem till they ben tender; than take hem up and pare hem, and kytte hem in to pecys; take ynow of powder of canel, a good quantyte, and caste it on red wyne, and draw it thorw a straynour; caste sugre ther-to, an put it an erthen pot, and let it boyle: an thanne caste the perys ther-to, and let boyle to-gederys, an whan they haue boye a whyle, take pouder of gyngere an caste ther-to, an a lytil venegre, an a lytil saffron; and loke that it be poynaunt an dowcet.

Ingredients:

2 lbs firm, ripe, unblemished pears (or 2 large cans of half pears)
2 cups red wine
½ cup sugar
2 tsp cinnamon
½ tsp ginger
1 Tbsp white vinegar

Desserts

Directions:

Fresh pears:

Poach the pears in a large pot of boiling water for about 5 minutes. (The easiest way to do this is to use one of those combination pasta and boiling pans, and put the pears in the pasta basket. Failing that, put a metal colander in the pot and blanch the pears in the colander. Lift the basket or colander out, and the pears come with.) Cool, peel and cut in half, removing cores and stems.

In an enamelled or non-stick pan (not aluminum, as it will discolor the pears), mix the cinnamon, sugar and wine, and warm until just about to boil. Gently place the pear halves in the mixture and simmer for about 10 minutes. (The lower heat keeps the pears from falling apart.)

In the last 2 minutes of cooking, remove ½ cup of the liquid, stir in the ginger and vinegar, and return to the pot, stirring gently around the pears.

Remove the pears, place cut side down in serving dishes. Pour the syrup over them and allow to cool together.

Canned pears:

Remove the pears from the liquid they are packed in. Place pears cut side down, one per serving dish.

Mix the wine, sugar and cinnamon together. Boil for 5 minutes, then reduce heat and simmer until it thickens. Add the ginger and vinegar, stir well, and cook for a minute or two more. Pour the syrup over the pears and allow to cool.

(If you refrigerate the pears for more than an hour, cover with plastic wrap to keep them from picking up odors.) Serve with one or two whole cloves studded in the pear halves.

a Man Stirring a 3-Legged Pot

Wardonys in Syryp (Pears in Wine Syrup) Traveling Dysshes

❖ Strawberye (Strawberry Pudding)

Gwyneth Felton and Serena Holmes, Two Fifteenth-Century Cookery-Books Harleian 279.123, 1430, England and France

This is a delightful dessert, and one that does well at a dance ball or tourney where your diners will be wandering in and out for small tastes of this or that. If you must make do with modern service vessels for this dish, 6 ounce plastic cocktail cups are a good choice, to keep the portion control on your side. Strawberye is also very yummy as a modern sauce for Cheesecake, too. Keep a light hand with the spices. Do not use an aluminum pan to cook this, as it will discolor the mixture and give the dessert a peculiar taste.

Serves 4 at home, 5-6 at an event.

Original:

Take Strawberys, & wasshe them in tyme of zere in gode red wyne; than strayne thorwe a clothe, & do hem in a potte wit god Almaunde mylke, a-lye it with Amyndoun other with the flowre of Ryse, & make it chargeaunt and lat it boyle, and do ther-in Roysonys of couraunce, Safroun, Pepir, Sugre great plente, pouder Gyngere, Canel, Galyngale, poynte it with Vynegre, & and lytil whyte grece put ther-to; coloure it with Alkenade, & droppe it abowte, plante it with the graynys of Pome-garnad, & than serue it forth.

Ingredients:

1 pint fresh strawberries (if you must use frozen, reserve the liquid to use instead
    of water in the recipe)
¼-1/2 cup red wine
¼ cup ground almonds
1/3 cup sugar
2 Tbsp rice flour
1 ¼ cup water (or juice from frozen berries)
pinch cinnamon, ginger, salt, pepper (remember, a *pinch*)
2 Tbsp currants
1 Tbsp butter
2 tsp wine vinegar

Desserts 127

Directions:

Hull and clean the strawberries. Leaving them whole, put in a large mixing bowl and pour the wine over them. Stir with your hand or a plastic spoon for about 5 minutes. Pour off and discard the wine. (If you are using frozen berries, thaw, reserve the juice, then mix the berries with the wine.)

Using a food mill, blender, or food processor, blend together the berries, almonds, cornstarch, sugar, spices and water.

In a medium enameled or non-stick saucepan bring the mixture to a boil over medium heat, stirring constantly with a wooden or plastic spoon. Let it boil for about 2 minutes, or until it thickens slightly. Do not over-boil.

Remove from heat at once and stir in the butter, then the vinegar and currants.

Pour into a large serving dish or individual dishes, and let cool. Serve chilled.

an Illustration from "The Canterbury Tales"

Strawberye (Strawberry Pudding)　　　　　　　Traveling Dysshes

❖ Creme Boyled (Custard Pudding)

Siobhan fidhlair, Two Fifteenth-Century Cookery-Books, 1430-1450, England and France

The bread in this recipe acts as a thickening agent, and the result is a lovely smooth pudding with a nice eggy, custardy taste.

Serves 6-8 at a potluck, 4 as a dessert.

Original:

Take creme or mylke, and brede of paynemayne, or ellys of tendre brede, and breke it on the creme, or elles in the mylke, an set it on the fyre tyl it be warm hot; and thorw a straynour throwe it, and put it into a fayre potte, an sette it on the fyre, an stere euermore: an whan it is almost yboylyd, take fair yolkes of eyron, an draw hem thorw a straynowr and caste hem ther-to, and let hem stonde ouer the fyre tyl it boyle almost, an till it be skylfully thikke; than caste a ladel-ful, or more or lasse, of boter ther-to, an a good quantite of whyte sugre, and a litel salt, an than dresse it on a dysshe in maner of mortrewys.

Ingredients:

5-10 slices of torn-up white bread
6 Tbsp melted butter
1 tsp salt
1 quart half-and-half
½ cup sugar
8 beaten egg yolks

Directions:

Soak bread in milk. Heat to hot but not boiling. Process until smooth, return to pot, heat again. Stir constantly; when almost boiling, stir in egg yolks. Continue to heat and stir, but don't boil until the pudding is thick. Remove from heat, stir in butter, sugar, and salt, and serve in bowls.

Currants

Desserts

❖ Daryoles (Custard Tart)

Siobhan Medhbh, Forme of Cury, 1390, England and France

These are custard tarts, with or without fruit. They make excellent individual tarts for dessert tables as well as one large tart (about 9") for a single table.

Original:

Take Creme of Coew milke, other of Almands, do therto ayren with suger, safron, and salt; medle it yfere; do it in a coffyn of ii. ynche depe, bake it wel and serue it forth.

Ingredients:

shortcrust pastry for a 9" pie or 12 tarts, unbaked
2 cups light cream
4 eggs
½ cup sugar
¼ tsp salt
pinch each of saffron, mace, nutmeg
¼ tsp almond extract
¾ cup chopped dates or fresh strawberries (optional)

Directions:

Beat eggs and sugar together until thick and glossy. Beat in cream and seasonings until well blended and foamy.

If you want to put fruit in your tarts, place it in the bottom of your unbaked pieshell.

Pour the custard mixture (onto the fruit) in the pastry shell. For a large tart, bake at 450 degrees F. for 10 minutes, then for 30 minutes at 300 degrees.

For individual tarts, bake about 20 minutes at 400 degrees F.

The tart mixture will puff when cooked, then fall when cooling. Serve cool or chilled.

130

❖ Per Fare Tortiglione Ripieno (Yeast Cake Stuffed with Raisins)

Siobhan Medhbh, Bartolomeo Scappi, Opera, Italy, between 1540 and 1570

This sweet cake, which could be made either as a large desert or small individual items, has a rich fruity filling and light yeasty bread. Because of the length it looks intimidating, but it really is easy.

Serves 1 (or two if they are friendly or on a diet).

Original:

Knead together 2 pounds of flour, 6 egg yolks, 2 ounces rose water, 1 ounce yeast dissolved in lukewarm water, and 4 ounces fresh butter or lard that does not smell bad, and quite a bit of salt, for half an hour so that the dough is well worked, and then roll it out thinly and cover it with melted butter that is not too hot, or lard, and with the pastry wheel cut all round the edges of the dough that are always thicker than the rest; sprinkle the dough with 4 ounces sugar, and 1 ounce cinnamon, and then have a pound of raisins that have been boiled in wine, and 1 pound of dates also cooked in wine and finely chopped, and one pound of seedless raisins boiled in wine, all mixed together with sugar, cinnamon, cloves, and nutmeg, and roll up the dough lengthwise like crêpes, being careful not to break the dough, and this tortiglione must not be rolled up more than three turns so that it cooks better, nor handled too much, but then basted with melted butter that is not too hot, then beginning from one end roll it up lightly like a snail or a maze, and have a pie pan prepared with a sheet of the same dough, of the same thickness, basted with butter. And put it lightly over the tortiglione without pressing it down, and cook in the oven in a moderate heat, basting with butter from time to time, and when it is cooked sprinkle with sugar, rose water, and serve hot. The pie pan used for the tortiglione should be open and with low sides.

Ingredients:

For the Dough:
½ oz compressed yeast
½ cup lukewarm water
1 tsp sugar
3 ½ cups flour
½ tsp salt
3 egg yolks
2 Tbsp rosewater
¼ tsp melted butter

Desserts

For the Filling:
¾ cup raisins
¾ cup currants
¾ cup pitted chopped dates
1 cup sweet white wine
½ cup sugar
1 Tbsp ground cinnamon
1/3 cup butter, melted for brushing
¼ cup butter, cut in small pieces

For the Glaze:
1 Tbsp rosewater
1 Tbsp fine sugar

Churning Butter

Directions:

To make the dough.
　Crumble the yeast into the warm water. Mix gently with the sugar, ¼ cup of the flour, and the egg yolks. Let it stand for 10 minutes or until it forms a sponge.
　Sift the flour and salt into a large bowl and make a well in the center. Add the rosewater, melted butter, and the yeast sponge and stir to form a smooth dough. Turn out onto a lightly floured board and knead until the dough is smooth and elastic, about 5-10 minutes.
　Put the dough in a lightly oiled bowl, turn over and over so that the dough is oiled on top. Cover with a damp cloth and leave in a warm place to rise until doubled in bulk, about 1 ½ hours.

To make the filling.
　Simmer the fruit in the wine, nutmeg, ¼ cup sugar, and cinnamon. Let the mixture simmer together until the fruit is plump and the wine is absorbed. This takes 10-15 minutes. Do not overboil. When the fruit has plumped up, take the mixture off the heat and let it cool.

To make the pastry.
　When the dough is risen, knead it lightly to knock the air out. Set aside a golf-ball sized lump for later use.
　Roll out the remaining dough thinly (1/4 inch) into a rectangle, about 12 x 18 inches. Trim the edges, holding the extra for decorations. Cut the rectangle in half.
　Thickly brush the remaining sugar mixed with the remaining cinnamon on the dough rectangles.

(Yeast Cake Stuffed with Raisins)　　　　　　　Traveling Dysshes

Spread the cooled fruit mixture on the dough, leaving about 1" at the top with no fruit. Dot the filling with pieces of butter. Roll the dough as if it were a crepe. You should be able to roll it only about 3 turns. Handle the dough carefully, making sure not to put your fingers through the dough.

Curl one of the rolls into a skillet, pushing it to the outside, with the seal down. Curl the other roll into the inside of the skillet, seal down. Form the two rolls into a yin-yang or other interlocking spiral.

Roll out the reserved dough to the same thickness (1/4 inch) as the original rectangle. Cut a circle the same size as your skillet. Cover the spiral with the dough, tucking the circle down loosely. Brush with butter and sprinkle with cinnamon and sugar.

With the trimmings, roll out another circle of the same size. Cover the first circle with the second, brushing with butter. Tuck it down into the pan, but do not push down on the filling inside.

Use the trimmings to make a decoration for the top. I choose to use a bunch of grapes, because of the raisins in the filling.

Brush with butter. Let it sit in a warm place to rise for about 30-40 minutes.

Preheat the oven to 375 degrees F.

Brush the dough with egg yolk and water if you like.

Bake the cake in the preheated oven for 20 minutes. You may want to put a tray or pan under the cake to catch the drippings.

Then turn down the heat to 325 degrees F. and cook until well browned, about 20 minutes. Brush twice with melted butter while it finishes cooking.

When you bring it from the oven, sprinkle with the rosewater and sugar. Serve hot.

a Grape Vine

Desserts

❖ Erbowle (Fresh Plum Pudding)

Siobhan Medhbh, Pleyn Delit, 2ⁿᵈ edition. Heiatt, Hosington, and Butler
This is a very easy, very yummy dish that travels well and is very pretty to prepare. It makes about 3 cups of finished product.

Original:

Take bolas and scald hem with wyne and drawe hem with a straynour do hem in a pot, clarify hony and do therto with powdor fort, and flor of Rys. Salt it & florish it w whyte aneys, & srve it forth.

Ingredients:

1 lb ripe fresh plums
1 cup each red wine and water
1/4 cup clear honey
1/4 tsp each salt, cinnamon
1/8 tsp each ginger, mace
1/4 cup rice flour, stirred into 1/4 cup cold water
10-15 whole roasted almonds

Directions:

Put plums in a saucepan and cover with wine and water; bring to a boil, and simmer 5 minutes (or until all the skins have turned lighter, and no darker, hard spots remain). Remove the plums and let cool 10 minutes. Keep the cooking liquid hot in the pan on the stove. Peel the plums and discard the pits. In a food processor or fruit sieve, puree the plums. Combine with honey and spices. Blend well.

Stir this pureed mixture back into the hot cooking liquid. Put the water in a jar with a tight lid; add the rice flour by sprinkling over the water. Cap the lid and shake vigorously. Pour slowly into the hot pudding, stirring continuously over medium heat. Continue until the pudding is quite thick (5-10 minutes). If there are lumps, reblend or sieve.

Pour into the serving dish (or dishes). Cool. When cool, chill. Garnish with whole almonds just before serving.

❖ Quaking Pudding (Batter Pudding)

Siobhan Medhbh, Elinor Fettiplace's Receipt Book
This is a dish, like "Lost Bread" (French toast), that has come down to us almost unchanged. It's still featured on menus in fine Scottish and French restaurants, and you can add almost any fruit or flavor into it. This recipe is in Elinor Fettiplace, but there are others in the literature, each a little different. Serves 8.

Original:

Take 6 ounces of fine flour, a little salt and 3 eggs, beat up well with a little milk, added by degrees till the batter is quite smooth, make it the thickness of cream, put into a buttered pie dish and bake three-quarters of an hour, or into a buttered and floured basin tied over tight with a cloth boil one and a half or two hours. Serve with an orange sweet syrup.

Ingredients:

3 oz (weight) flour
3 oz (weight) fine white breadcrumbs
pinch salt
3 eggs, beaten
1 cup cream or half and half
1/8 tsp nutmeg
3-4 Tbsp mixed currants and raisins

Directions:

Mix the flour and breadcrumbs in a bowl, and make a well in the middle. Drop in the beaten eggs and work into a batter with a wooden or plastic spoon.

Add the cream little by little, beating well. Then stir in the fruit and nutmeg.

Put in a well-greased dish and bake for 45 minutes at 350 degrees F. until it is well risen and browned. Serve at once with Orange-Butter Sauce.

❖ Orange-Butter Sauce

Ingredients:

½ cup melted butter
½ cup brown sugar
1 tsp orange extract or flower water

Directions:

Beat the sugar and butter together until foamy. Add the orange-flower water (or orange extract). Stir until creamy/rich looking, and serve immediately with the pudding.

Bees Drinking Mead

❖ A Flaune of Almayne (Mixed Fruit Pie)

Cariadoc and Elizabeth, Ancient Cookery, page 452

Note that the "almayne" in this title does not indicate that this is another almond recipe, but rather that this tart came from or is done in the style of Alemania, or Germany. Makes one 9" pie.

Original:

First take raisins of Courance, or else other fresh raisins, and good ripe pears, or else good apples, and pick out the cores of them, and pare them, and grind them, and the raisins in a mortar, and do then to them a little sweet cream of milk, and strain them through a clean strainer, and take ten eggs, or as many more as will suffice, and beat them well together, both the white and the yolk, and draw it through a strainer, and grate fair white bread, and do thereto a good quantity, and more sweet cream, and do thereto, and all this together; and take saffron, and powder of ginger, and canel, and do thereto, and a little salt, and a quantity of fair, sweet butter, and make a fair coffin or two, or as many as needs, and bake them a little in an oven, and do this batter in them, and bake them as you would bake flaunes, or crustades, and when they are baked enough, sprinkle with canel and white sugar. This is a good manner of Crustade.

Ingredients:

2/3 cup raisins
3 pears or apples
½ tsp cinnamon
¼ tsp ginger
pinch of saffron
½ tsp salt
3 eggs (large)
¼ cup breadcrumbs
½ cup whipping cream
5 Tbsp butter
9" pie crust
1 Tbsp cinnamon sugar to sprinkle on at the end

Directions:

A blender works well as a substitute for a mortar to mash the apples and raisins; mix the liquids (slightly beaten eggs and cream) in with the apples and raisins before blending in the spices and breadcrumbs. Put mixture in piecrust, dot top with cut up pieces of butter. Bake at 375 degrees F. for about an hour.

Desserts

❖ A Tart of Almonds (Almond Pie)

Cordelia Toser, The Good Huswives Handmaid, 1599.

Just before serving, Cordelia spreads half the cooled pie with a layer of strawberry preserves, because the fruit counterbalances the richness of the filling. That way, those who have less of a sweet tooth or who don't care for strawberries can avoid the fruit.

Serves 10-12.

Original:

Blanch almonds and beat them, and strain them fine with good thicke Creame. Then put in Sugar and Rosewater, and boyle it thicke. Then make your paste with butter, fair water, and the yolks of two or three Egs, and so soone as ye have driven your paste, cast on a little sugar, and rosewater, and harden your paste afore in the oven. Then take it out, and fill it, and set it in againe, and let it bake till it be wel, and so serve it.

Ingredients:

9 inch pie shell, unbaked
2 cups blanched almonds, coarsely ground
2 cups heavy cream
5 tsp sugar
5 tsp rosewaer
small jar of strawberry preserves (optional)

Directions:

Bake pie shell at 425 degrees F for 10 minutes, remove pie shell from oven and cool. Reduce oven temperature to 350.

Combine almonds, cream, sugar and rosewater in heavy saucepan. Cook gently about 10 minutes, stirring occasionally, until mixture thickens a bit.

Pour filling into pie shell and bake for 30 minutes, or until top is golden. Cool pie to room temperature. Serve immediately or refrigerate.

Just before serving, spread layer of preserves on the pie.

a Knot

❖ Cryspes (Sweet Fried Dough)

Siobhan Medhbh, from Le Viandier, translation from French to English, taken from the Miscelleny

Even if you've never had funnel cakes at the fair, you have to try this recipe. Discovering that this period version of our modern harvest fair trest makes it a little easier to imagine the bustle and delight of a Market Day in town.

Original:

Take white of eyroun, milk, and flour, and a little berme, and beat it together, and draw it through a strainer, so that it be running, and not too stiff, and cast sugar thereto, and salt; then take a chafer full of fresh grease boiling, and put thine hand in the batter, and let thine batter run down by thy fingers into the chafer; and when it is run together on the chafer, and is enough, take and nym a skimmer, and take it up, and let all the grease run out, and put it on a fair dish, and cast thereon sugar enough, and serve forth

Ingredients:

4 egg whites
2/3 cup milk
1 cup flour
1 Tbsp dried yeast
3 Tbsp sugar
½ tsp salt

Directions:

Take egg white, milk, and flour and a little yeast and beat it together, being careful not to let the flour make lumps. Add sugar and salt. Pour into a pan of hot oil, so that they puff up and brown, turn them, drain them, sprinkle on sugar and serve them.

This can be done either as a pancake, or as something more like a funnel cake; the latter seems to fit the description more closely. To make it like a funnel cake, use a slotted spoon; the batter runs through the slots into the hot grease. Of course, you could always let thy batter run down by thy fingers instead, but make sure no one is watching.

a Cow & a Frog in Conversation

❖ A Fruit Pudding (Steamed Suet Pudding)

Siobhan Medhbh, The Good Huswives Handmaid, 1599.

This was a fun topic to research and develop, as steamed puddings, in and out of cloths, figure so prominently in European meals for the last 1000 years or more. It's a great way to cook a healthy, nourishing treat without having a lot of metal pans around to cook in, and can be made in a kettle if no oven is available. Serves 6-8 at a feast table, 4-5 at home.

Original:

Three or four dayes before you wish to serve, soak the cooked fruit in spices and wine or brandy. Let it stepe for 2 days, in a cool place and cover'd. On the day of baking, drain the liquor. Grate fat within, also the peels of lemon and orange, and combine further with flour, a goodly lump of sugar, and eggs. Press into a fine cloth within a dish, and steam until hardened.

Ingredients:

1 lb mixed dried fruit
Water to cover
3/4 cup brandy
2 tsp cinnamon
1 tsp allspice
2 tsp mace
1 1/2 tsp nutmeg
1/4 lb suet or lard, grated
3 Tbsp grated orange peel
2 Tbsp grated lemon peel
1/4 cup flour
3 eggs, beaten
1/2 cup white sugar

Directions:

Cut the dried fruit in bite-sized pieces and cover it with water. Bring to a boil and let simmer for about an hour. Pour everything into a ceramic or hard plastic bowl. Add the brandy, spices, and 2 tsp of the sugar. Cover the bowl tightly, and refrigerate for 48 hours.

In a large mixing bowl, grate the lard or suet (this works much better if the fat is frozen in advance), and cream together with the peels, flour, and remaining sugar. Mix in the beaten eggs well.

Drain the fruit and stir into the rest.

Grease your steaming tins well with butter and coat with fine white sugar. Press the mixture in until the tins are 2/3 full. Cover tightly.

Desserts 141

Steam in a kettle on a tripod. When you place the tin(s) within the kettle, the water should be boiling vigorously. The water level should be below the bottom of the tins but there should be at least 1-2 inches of water in the kettle. Close the kettle tightly.

Boil vigorously for 8-10 minutes, and then turn the heat down so that the water boils gently. If you have one large tin, steam for about 3 hours. (Add more boiling water from the kettle if necessary.) Small tins should steam for about 1 ¼ to 1 ½ hours.

When the time is up, take the steaming tins out of the kettle immediately. Open the lids so that the excess steam within can escape and cool for about 10 minutes. Turn the tins over on a serving dish and let them sit for a few minutes, then gently lift the tins off the puddings.

Serve hot or cold with sauce.

[Note: If you wish to boil the pudding, use a large piece of clean cheesecloth. Spread the cloth out on a large baking sheet. Pile the pudding batter about 1/3 of the way in from one long edge of the cloth, in a loaf-shape about 10 inches long. Starting from the side closest to the pudding mixture, fold the cloth over the pudding and then roll the remaining cloth up around the pudding. Twist the ends tightly and tie with a strong string. If the pudding looks like it will leak out of the cloth, wrap again in a second cloth. If the pudding looks like it will leak out of the cloth, wrap again in a second cloth. Twist the ends tightly and tie firmly.

Boil a kettle of water. Gently place the bundled pudding in the water, which should cover it fully. Boil vigorously for about 10 minutes, then reduce to an energetic simmer for another hour, or until the pudding feels firm when you poke it with a blunt spoon. Boil for up to one more hour if necessary.

Remove from the water and then remove the cloth.]

a Basket of Figs

A Fruit Pudding (Steamed Suet Pudding)   Traveling Dysshes

Menus

One of the goals for this book is that everyone who plays in the SCA will know how to cook one period dish, or how to go shopping and show up at a potluck or camping event with a period contribution.

Many of you will soon branch out to cooking whole meals, and will wonder about what should constitute a good menu.

There are many examples of period menus to be had. Many of the cookbooks and source books listed in the resource section also include real menus.

One of the most amusing is Robert May's "Feast for Christmas Day" from *The Accomplisht Cook,* published early in the 1600's.

Feast for Christmas Day

The first Course

- ❖ Oysters
- ❖ A Collar of Brawn
- ❖ Stewed Broth of Mutton marrow bones
- ❖ A grand Sallet
- ❖ A Pottage of Caponets
- ❖ A Breast of Veal in Stoffado
- ❖ A Boil'd Partridge
- ❖ A chine of Beef, or surloin roast
- ❖ Minced pies
- ❖ A jegote of mutton with anchovie sauce
- ❖ A made dish of sweet-bread
- ❖ A swan roast
- ❖ A pasty of venison
- ❖ A kid with a pudding in his belly
- ❖ A steak pie
- ❖ A haunch of Venison roasted
- ❖ A turkey roast and stuck with cloves
- ❖ A made dish of chickens in puff paste
- ❖ Two bran geese roasted, one larded
- ❖ Two large capons, one larded
- ❖ A Custard

The Second Course for the Same Mess

- Oranges and Lemons
- A young lamb or kid
- Two couple of rabbits, two larded
- A pig souc'd with tongues
- Three ducks, one larded
- Three pheasants, one larded
- A Swan Pye
- Three brace of Partridge, three larded
- Made dish in Puff Paste
- Bolonia sausages, and anchovies, and pickled oysters in a dish, with mushrooms and Caviare
- Six teals, three larded
- A Gammon of Westphalia Bacon
- Ten ploves, five larded
- Aquince pye or warden pye
- Six woodcocks, three larded
- A Standing tarte in puff paste, preserved fruits, pippins,&c.
- A dish of larks
- Six dried neat's tongues
- Sturgeon
- Powdered Geese (yes, that's what it says)
- Jellies.

Whew! Luckily, no one expects this to turn up at a camp feast or in our feast halls!

Caxton's Rendering of the Feast in the Canterbury Tales

Menu Planning Help Online

There is lots of help available to help you plan menus. Some of the best comes from folks who have been doing this for a while. Luckily, many of them are publishing their recipes on the Internet these days. A good online resource, not only for menus but also for general cooking, is hosted by the Ministry of Arts and Sciences in Atlantia. You can find it at:
http://moas.atlantia.sca.org/topics/cook.htm

Stefan's Florilegium, a monumental resource for the SCA participant, has another good index to period menus, available at:
http://www.florilegium.org/files/FEASTS/idxfeasts.html

Another really excellent source online is the Book of Gode Cookery, which has tons of resources, including menu suggestions. Find it at:
http://www.godecookery.com

a Vintner Checking the Clarity of His Wine

Sample Menus

Finally, here are some samples for you from feasts Cordelia and Siobhan have prepared or assisted with. We'll not only list the dishes and courses, but try to talk about the rationale for the choices.

Golden Rivers Anniversary Feast 2000

This feast was designed as a self challenge for Siobhan — to prepare a whole feast from a single source, if at all possible. *Le Menagier* was the source chosen. We also intended to try and find fun, new recipes — things the local feast audience wasn't used to. The fried cheese and "funnel cakes" were a big hit.

Table Course

(Waiting on the table when folks enter, to facilitate mingling and also hold off the ravenous hordes if something is running late!)
- Manchet and butter
- Pykels and savories
- Stuffed Tubes

First Course

- Two Chikens from One
- Cryspes
- Cress in Lent with Milk of Almonds

Second Course

- Bourbelier of Fresh Boar
- Frumenty
- Green Egg and Cheese Soup

Desserts

- Darioles
- A Flaune of Almayne
- Baked Applis

a Goose

A Twelfth Night Feast for the American Recorder Society

The American Recorder Society has a Twelfth Night Celebration every year — for the past few years the SCA has been cooking the feast, to help promote better links with this group of musicians. Their feasts generally have to meet these criteria: Inexpensive enough to fit student budgets; mostly period but not required; easy to serve between 6:30 and 8 pm; and easy to clean up after. The menu below is typical; it cost $11.50 per head to purchase and prepare in 2002. Non-period items are marked with a *.

Table Course

- Cheeses (Havarti, Cheddar)
- Breads
- Butter
- Ham slices
- Fruit (orange sections)

First Course

- Roast Chicken
- Spinach Tart
- Buttered Carrots & parsnips
- Bread pudding & hard sauce *

Second Course

- Roast Pork
- Batter Pudding in butter and orange sauce
- Grene Beans
- Applesauce

Dessert

- Mincemeat Pie
- Strawberye Pudding
- Darioles
- Fools' Cake *

a Woman in a Headdress Stuffing a Chicken

Scottish Night Feast at Collegium Occidentalis, Fall 1999

This feast was at the event where Siobhan transitioned management of the Collegium to the new Regents. Advertising for the feast said, "In order to enable Rose and Juan to enjoy a smooth transition without Siobhan either having a panic attack or getting in their hair, Dame Siobhan Medhbh will be cooking the feast." Like the Golden Rivers feast, the intent was to try new recipes and explore a new cuisine. Some of the dishes skirt the edge of the SCA period, as they appeared in print around 1630. In some cases, we did some backtracking of recipes, looking at meals served in great houses of Scotland in the 1650's to 1700's, and seeing if we had period recipes available.

Table Course

- Smoked Salmon
- Cheeses & herbs
- Oatcakes

First Course:

- Bawd Bree (meat & vegetable soup)
- Forfar Bridies
- Caboges
- Pearsauce

Second Course:

- Roe Forcemeat (Venison Sausages)
- Skirlie
- Herbolet (cheese and vegetable tart)
- Carrets

Dessert:

- Shortbread
- Athol Brose pudding
- Bannock
- Plum Pudding

a Woman Carrying Produce to Market

Collett & Alessandro's Wedding

The task was to please the bride (a vegetarian), the groom (who wanted only foods known in Italy in period), the families of the bride and groom, neither of which are accustomed to historic dishes, and the bulk of the guests who are SCA. The meal was served buffet style starting around 3pm, to a crowd who had not had lunch. Red and white wines were served at table. [Note from Siobhan, who attended and ate but did not have to cook — it was scrumptious, and my date, who usually dislikes "period" meals, ate way too much.]

Food and beverages available when guests arrive

- ❖ Hard cheeses, sliced
- ❖ Fresh made cheeses with serving utensils
- ❖ Breads sliced
- ❖ Grapes and strawberries
- ❖ Hot water for tea
- ❖ Iced tea
- ❖ Ice water in pitchers
- ❖ Sugar and cream
- ❖ Various soft drinks

Food served half an hour after the bride and groom arrive

- ❖ Pasta with choice of pesto sauce, cream sauce, Agliata/garlic sauce
- ❖ Shredded mozzarella on the side
- ❖ Loseynes
- ❖ Three kinds of pie
    - o Tart on Ember Day
    - o Tarte of Spinnage (made non-diary for lactose intolerant guests)
    - o Pastry of Artichoke
- ❖ Garbanzo dish
- ❖ Funges (Mushrooms and leeks)
- ❖ Green salad with oil/vinegar dressing
- ❖ Fruit salad (apples, seedless grapes, red raspberries, etc.)
- ❖ Pastries stuffed with nuts and cinnamon sugar

Jingles Feast 1995

For many years, the Province of Southern Shores has begun the holiday season with a Jingles Feast. One year there were three chief cooks (Euriol of Lothian, Ivan Streltsov and Cordelia Toser), one for each course. (This is a sneaky way of showing someone that he/she really can put together a whole feast.)

The First Course was from Apicius

- Condimentum in Rubellionen (Red Snapper with Sauce)
- Aliter Cucumbers (Cucumbers, another Method)
- Conchicla de Pisa Simplici (A simple dish of peas)
- Caroetae Frictae (Fried Carrots)
- Pullus Tractogalatus (Chicken over pasta)
- Bread

The second course was Russian.

- Pomegranate Chicken Broth
- Wild Mushroom Caviar
- Beef Stroganoff
- Red Bean Pie
- Rye Bread
- Apple Baba

The third course was English.

- Jowtes of Almand Mylke
- Tart on an Ember Day (Onion/cheese tart)
- Rabbits in Syrup (Rabbits stewed in spiced wine)
- Rice
- Appulmoy (Applesauce)
- Shortbread

a Pair of Cake Knives

Sources

Thanks to Katerine (J. Terry Nutter), who provided annotations for many of these books in the first edition, and to Cordelia and Juana who have assisted with more for this volume.

Books & Websites with Modern Recipes

Austin, Thomas, *Two Fifteenth-Century Cookery-Books,* Early English Text Society. Original Series No. 91 (1884); reprinted with permission by Kraus Reprint, 1640. Probably the best single source of 15th century English cookery.

Beebe, Ruth Ann, *Sallets, Humbles, and Shrewsbury Cakes.* Boston, David R. Godine, 1976. ISBN 0-87923-195-5. This is an easy-to-read and easy to follow edition with recipes from several well-known Elizabethan cookbooks.

Black, Maggie, *The Medieval Cookbook.* Thames and Hudson, New York 1992. ISBN 0-500-01548-1. She uses recipes from a number of good sources, such as *Menagier de Paris.* A good book for a beginner in Medieval cooking.

De Nola, Ruperto, *Libro de Cozina,* 1529. Translated by Vincent F. Cuenca, 2001. Information on carving of meats and birds, the order in which beverages and foods should be served, the duties of the various offices of a noble household, the proper behavior of servants, and of course, lots of recipes. Unfortunately the original Spanish text is not included.

Dembińska, Maria, *Food and Drink in Medieval Poland.* Translated by Magdalena Thomas. ISBN 0-8122-3224-0. Well researched culinary information from a new part of Europe. Correct varieties of grains and vegetables are used. Recipes are conjectural, but well thought through.

Friedman, David, and Elizabeth Cook, *A Miscelleny,* 1988, 1990, 1992, 1996, 1998, 2000). This book contains Cariadoc and Elizabeth's recipe collection, plus a collection of articles and poems. Except for the recipes, everything is by Cariadoc unless stated otherwise. This is an exceptional first collection of recipes and practical hints for learning how to cook medieval food. Contact the author by email: ddfr@best.com, or by USPS at 3806 Williams Road, San Jose, CA 95117.

Hartley, Dorothy, *Food in England.* MacDonald and Jane's, London, 1975. ISBN 0-356-08302-0. Mostly out of period, but very useful and detailed information about food animals and plants available in the British Isles, some no longer commonly eaten, and food preparation methods used in prior-to-modern kitchens.

Hess, Karen, transcription. *Martha Washington's Booke of Cookery.* Columbus University Press, 1981, ISBN 0-231-04930-7. The age of these recipes is unclear, as they had been passed down through her family for generations;

Sources 151

however many recipes are recognizably from our period. Hess's copious notes, references to similar recipes in other cookbooks, and annotations are well worth reading. Renfrow's best estimate is that the bulk of the recipes come from the years *1550-1625.*

Hieatt, Constance B., *An Ordinance of Pottage.* London, Prospect Books, 1988. Ordinance is another work which combines scholarly information on period sources with easy, modern-kitchen recipes.

Hieatt, Constance B. and Sharon Butler, eds. *Cury on Inglysh.* Includes the complete ms. of *Forme of Cury.* London, Early English Text Society, 1985. ISBN 0-19-722409-1. This is a scholarly work containing not only translations of many recipes but annotations and comparisons on various versions of *Forme of Cury.* Along the other valuable resources in the volume, Hieatt and Butler include several sample menus from the era to help with feast planning. As always, Hieatt and Butler include lots of cultural and economic material as well as kitchen technology.

Hieatt, Constance B. and Sharon Butler, *Pleyn Delit.* Toronto, University of Toronto Press, 1976, 1979. Paperback 1979, 1985, 1987. ISBN 0-8020-6366-7. Like *Sallets, Humbles, Pleyn Delit* is a work for the modern cook who wants to explore medieval cooking. The original recipes are included as well as Hieatt and Butler's translations. This is an excellent resource for beginners as well as advanced cooks.

Hieatt, Constance B. and Sharon Butler, "Two Anglo-Norman Culinary Collections Edited from British Library Manuscripts Additional 32085 and Royal 12.C.xii," in *Speculum* v.61 #4 (1986), 859-881. These are originals and translations of the two earliest usable recipe collections currently known from England; one dates from the 13th century, the other from the early 14th.

Hodgett, Gerald A. J., *Stere Htt Well,* Cornmarket Reprints (London), 1972. This is a reprint of a volume originally published in the 19th century. It contains side-by-side a facsimile of a late 15th century collection of miscellaneous recipes and an edition from a later date. The reader should beware, as Hodgett clearly took liberties in editing. The title is pretty clearly a mis-typesetting of "Stere Hit Well", but when looking in on-line references, it is sometimes important to reproduce the typo.

Lorwin, Madge, *Dining with William Shakespeare.* Atheneum, New York, 1976. ISBN 0-689-10731-5. Pat, I will let someone else comment on this book, as I haven't used it much yet.

McKendry, Maxime (and Arabella Boxer, Editor). *Seven Hundred Years of English Cooking.* 1973, Treasure Press, London. 240 pages. This volume has a vast number of historical recipes spanning from the fourteenth century to the twentieth. While some of the recipes are obviously modified for modern tastes, McKendry is scrupulous in including the period source of each recipe and the original recipe with each translation.

Books & Websites with Modern Recipes   Traveling Dysshes

Matterer, James L, *A Boke of Gode Cookery*.1997-2002, http://www.godecookery.com/gcooktoc/gcooktoc.htm . This is an exceptional site to use as a master-hub for many, many cookbooks, with strict attention to attribution, research, and a broad reach of available period sources.

Morris, Richard, *Liber Cure Cocorum*, Asher and Co. for the Philological Society (1885). This is one of the earliest books (the volume for 1862-1864) in the Philological Society's Early English Volume series, which later became the Early English Text Society series. It occurs in this volume along with *Hampole's Pricke of Conscience* and *The Castel off Loue*. The manuscript itself dates from about 1440, and is a collection of culinary recipes in rhymed verse.

Redon, Sabban & Serventi, *The Medieval Kitchen, Recipes from France and Italy*. Translated by Edward Schneider. University of Chicago Press, 1998. ISBN 0-226-70684-2.

Renfrow, Cindy, *A Sip Through Time.* 1995, 1996, 1997, Renfrow. ISBN 0-9628598-3-4. A collection of over 400 old brewing recipes, as early as Pliny the Elder.

Renfrow, Cindy. *Take a Thousand Eggs or More: A Collection of 15th Century Recipes*, Vols. 1 & II. 1990, Renfrow. ISBN 0-9628598-1-8. Renfrew has both the original sources and the redactions, as well as discussions of the serving, tables, and kitchens. In the Society for Creative Anachronism, Cindy Renfrew is known as Mistress Sincgiefu Waerfaest. This book is available through the Society Stock Clerk.

Santich, Barbara, *The Original Mediterranean Cuisine*. Chicago Review Press, Chicago, IL, 1995. ISBN 1-55652-272-X. Easy to follow recipes. Pat, unfortunately my language skills are not sufficient to critique her translations. cns

Sass, Lorna J., *To the King's Taste.* The Metropolitan Museum of Art. 1975. ISBN 0-87099-133-7. Most recipes are from the Forme of Cury, written about 1390 for Richard II of England.

Sass, Lorna J., *To the Queen's Taste.* The Metropolitan Museum of Art (Sadly, my copy is missing the publication date.) Recipes from English cookery books published between 1550 and 1620. Historical information about food and dining customs of the time.

Scully, D. Eleanor & Terence Scully, *Early French Cookery*. University of Michigan Press, Ann Arbor, MI, 1995. ISBN 0-472-10648-1. Well tested recipes, sometimes a combination of multiple originals. The translations from medieval French are fairly accurate.

Scully, Terence, ed. Chiquart's *On Cookery: a fifteenth century Savoyard culinary treatise*. New York: P. Lang, c1986, xlv, 138 pages.

Scully, Terence, ed. *The Viandier of Taillevent*. Ottawa, University of Ottawa Press, 1988.

Willan, Anne. *Great Cooks and Their Recipes, from Taillevent to Escoffier.* 1997, 1992, Bullfinch Press, Boston, 224 pages, including 100 color plates. This is a beautiful book, including wonderful plates with elegant presentations of many of the recipes. The historical and cultural environment for each of the cooks is briefly explained. While not an extensive resource, it's worth having.

W., *A Book of Cookrye*, London, 1591. Originally published 1584. STC 24897 -- Early English Text microfilms reel 1613:9, transcribed by Mark and Jane Waks.

a Nurse Feeding a Child

Sources with Only Medieval Recipes

Dawson, Thomas, *The Good Huswifes Jewell* 1596 and The Second Part of the Good Hus-wives Jewell 1597. Falconwood Press, Albany, NY. 1988.

Digby, Kenelme, *The Closet of the Eminently Learned Sir Kenelme Digby Kt. Opened.* (1669) edited by Jane Stevenson and Peter Davidson, Prospect Books, Devon. 1997. ISBN 0907325-79. The text is that published by Brome in London, 1669. Another posthumous collection of recipes, including a huge selection of meads and mead-like recipes; one of the best early sources for brewing. Roughly half is dedicated to brewing, the other half to culinary recipes. Most of the recipes are clearly earlier than the late date on the book indicates; Digby collected them, and he died in 1665. Also available through the UMI Early English Books microfilm series; this reproduction is in excellent shape, and easy to read.

Faccioli, Emilio, ed. *Arte della cucina.* 2 vols. Contains the full-text edition of Martino ms. and other Italian ms. Rome, Edizione il Polifilo, 1966.

Les Fine Herbs. *Medieval Fayre.* 1980, privately published.

Markham, Gervase, *The English hous-wife: containing the inward and outward vertues which ought to be in a compleat woman*, Sixth Edition, E. Brewster and George Sawbridge (London) 1656. A collection which includes culinary and other material. Markham himself was born in 1568 and died in 1637; however, the edition claims to be "augmented", so the recipes may not all be as early as he was. Available through the UMI Early English Books microfilm series; this reproduction is in excellent shape, and easy to read.

May, Robert, *The Accomplisht Cook*, Prospect Books, Devon. 1994. ISBN 0907325-54-8. First published in 1660 late in May's life, this is a facsimile of the 1685 edition. A good overview of English and French cooking in the first half of the 17th century. Very good baking information. Excellent glossary.

Murrell, John, *Delightful daily exercise for ladies and gentlemen.* Private. Photocopy from the MSU collection. 1621.

Partridge, John, *The Treasurie of commodious Conceits, & hidden Secrets.* Richard Jones (London) 1573. A collection of miscellaneous recipes, including many for preserves and candied fruits, as well as medicinals, recipes for perfuming gloves and clothes, and other miscellany. Available through the UMI Early English Books microfilm series, the original from which the microfilm was made was poorly printed, with smudges and bleed through, and is unfortunately difficult to read.

Prescott, James, tr. *le Viandier de Taillevent.* 1987, 1988, 1989. Alfahaugr Publishing Society, Eugene, Oregon. Prescott's version of le Viandier is excellently done, and includes one of the best glossaries of French cooking terms I've seen.

Platt, Hugh, *Delightes for Ladies, to adorne their Persons, Tables, closets, and distillatories: with Beauties, banquest, perfumes, and Waters*. Peter Short (London) 1602. One of the best early sources for confections and for distilled preparations (many not alcoholic: things like rosewater and other flavored and scented water), as well as an excellent source of culinary recipes. Available through the UMI Early English Books microfilm series; this reproduction is in excellent shape, and easy to read.

Platina, *On Right Pleasure and Good Health*. Translation by Mary Ella Milham. The Renaissance Society of America, Vol. 17. Tempe, AZ, 1998. ISBN 0-86698-208-6. The Latin and English texts are on facing pages. Platina's life, originality, and friends are also discussed.

Spurling, Elinor Fettiplace's Receipt Book, ISBN 0-670-81592-6, 1992. This is a fabulous book with lots of good information about later period household management.

Weber, Shirley Howard, *Anthimus, De Observatio Ciborum*. E. J. Brill Ltd, Leiden 1924.

The Pope Crowns a Pig

Books about Food & Cooking

Hagen, Ann. *A Handbook of Anglo-Saxon Food Processing and Consumption.* 1994, Anglo-Saxon Books, Middlesex, England. ISBN 0-9516209-8-3. While academic and therefore sometimes rather dry, the wealth of information about food, customs, and household operation in Anglo-Saxon times is astonishing.

Hammond, P.W., *Food and Feast in Medieval England.* Sutton Publishing, Stroud, Gloucestershire, 1998. ISBN 0-905-778-251. Discusses food availability in town and country, adulteration and nutrition, table manners, and feasts.

McGee, Harold. *On Food and Cooking.* 1986, Collier, New York. *The Curious Cook.* 1990, Collier, New York. McGee's books translate food chemistry and physics into normal human language, as well as tips and hints about handling and preparing food. They are filled with literary lore and historic anecdotes.

Rombauer, Irma S., Marion Rombauer Becker and Ethan Becker. *The All New All Purpose Joy of Cooking.* Simon & Schuster, New York. 1997. ISBN 0-683-81870-1. Joy is a classic work from which to learn many basic techniques in the kitchen.

Root, Waverly, *Food.* Smithmark Publishers, New York, 1980. ISBN 88-88551-96-4. An encyclopedia of articles about foods and their history. He states when and where foods were originally found and quotes other authorities who may not agree, which allows the reader to draw his own conclusions.

Scully, Terence, *The Art of Cookery in the Middle Ages.* Boydell & Brewer Ltd, Rocheester, NY ISBN 0-85115-430-1, 1995 The lore and logic of the noble kitchens of Europe in the fourteenth and fifteenth centuries is explored and commented on. All of Scully's books are very informative and entertaining.

Tannahay, Reay. *Food in History.* 1988, Crown Trade Paperbacks, New York. Tannahill's guide is not the most authoritative, but it is entertaining and informative, and more often than not, accurate.

Toussant-Samat, Maguelonne, *History of Food.* Translated by Anthea Bell. Blackwell Publishers, Cambridge, MA. 1994, 1996.ISBN 0-631-19497-5. Fascinating reading, beginning with the most ancient legendary information on various foods, gardens, orchards, and food preserving methods.

Recipes Removed from the first edition

There were a number of recipes in the first edition that we have not been able to track back to the original recipe. Consequently, we are uncomfortable presenting them as a period recipe, especially when more and more people are using this book as documentation for contest entries! Others were so radically different from the original manuscript that we have either re-translated them or are not certain of the provenance. However, many of our readers really like these recipes, and to oblige them we have kept them, but moved them back to this section to clearly point out their uncertain origins.

❖ Braun (Roast Pork in Dry Marinade)

Siobhan Medhbh, le Viandier de Taillevent 1375-90, France
This dish stays moist and tender without basting or much tending at all. It's best when it's *shlumpf,* or falling to pieces.

Original:

(I'm sure I found this in Taillevent, but can't find the original source. ☹)

Ingredients:

3-4 lb boneless pork roast, rolled and tied
1/2 cup each parsley flakes, dried onion, oregano, rosemary, sage, thyme
2 Tbsp powdered ginger
1 Tbsp powdered mace

Directions:

Mix the spices together in a flat pan. Roll the roast in it until well covered. Roast for 20 minutes per pound at 350 degrees F., or until a meat thermometer shows 160 degrees.

❖ Mincemeat Tart

Ingredients:

1 oz can tart apple pie filling
1 oz package mixed dried fruit (apples, raisins, pears, etc.)
1 oz package chopped dates
1 oz package currants
1/4 lb butter
2 cups water
1 cup brown sugar
1 cup orange juice
1 cup lemon juice
½ tsp each nutmeg, cinnamon
¼ tsp mace
1 tsp salt
1 tsp lemon peel, grated
4 pie shells, 9 inch

Directions:

Mix all the ingredients in a saucepan except pie shells. Cook over medium heat until it starts to boil, then reduce heat to low and simmer until all the dried fruit has plumped and gotten soft.

Fill the pie shells. Cook for 20 minutes in a 350 degree F. oven or until shell is browned. Serve with Brandy Hard Sauce.

❖ Brandy Hard Sauce

Ingredients:

2 cups powdered sugar
½ cup soft butter
1 tsp brandy
1 egg yolk, beaten
1 egg white, beaten

Directions:

Stir butter and sugar together until creamy. Add brandy, slowly. Stir in egg yolk; fold in egg white. Chill. Serve with hot or cool pie.

Recipes Removed from the first edition

❖ Spinage Tart (Spinach Tart)

Ingredients:

2 pie shells, 9 or 10 inch
1 lb cheese, grated (mixed cheddar and jack is pleasant)
4 eggs
1 (10 oz.?) package frozen, chopped spinach
2 cups milk, cream, half-n-half, or sour cream, or a mixture of all
pinch salt
pinch nutmeg

Directions:

Thaw the spinach and break it up. Mix with the cheese. Mound half the spinach and cheese in each pie.

Mix the eggs, milk (or cream), and spices well until they form a custard. Pour half over contents of each pie shell. The liquid will pool up under the vegetable and cheese.

Bake for 15 minutes at 425 degrees F. Turn oven down to 350 and cook for 35-45 minutes more, or until custard puffs up and starts to brown, and middle is set. Serve warm or cold.

Also good with other greens or vegetables.

❖ Fruit Tarts

These tiny tarts are wonderful carry-along desserts, and can be made from whatever jellies, jams, or marmalades you have in the house. Serena Holmes and Gwyneth Felton use the "all-fruit" varieties currently on the market for a less processed result.

Ingredients:

shortcrust pastry for 12 tarts
12 oz fruit marmalade, jelly, or jam

Directions:

Make 12 tart shells, and bake for 10 minutes in a 350 degree oven (or until lightly browned). Put 2 Tbsp (about 1 ounce) of fruit in each tart. Return to the oven for 5 minutes, or until the mixture just begins to bubble.

Index

A Dysshe of Artichokes 86
A Flaune of Almayne.............158
A Fruit Pudding 162
A Recipe for a Dish of Chicken
 or Partridge with Quince or
 Apple 116
A Tart of Almonds 159
Acceptable.......................16, 19
Alawder de beef...................123
Aliper...............................25, 27
Almond Milk....................44, 85
Almond Pie...........................159
Aloes of Beef 123
Apples....20, 39, 49, 70, 76, 116,
 158
Applesauce.................23, 25, 76
Artichokes 19, 86
Auter Tartus 69
Balsalmic vinegar 131
Batter Pudding.....................156
Beans....................20, 24, 33, 87
Beef...19, 23, 25, 27, 33, 37, 48,
 53, 64, 82, 95, 108, 120, 123,
 134
Beef, Chicken, & Hard Boiled
 Egg Pie...............................64
Beet 19, 78, 85, 92, 99
Benes y-Fride 87
Berries....................................20
Beverages.......................22, 142
Blood......................................37
Blueberries.............................20
Boar.................................25, 37
Books...................................172
Bor in Counfett.....................121
Bourbelier of Fresh Boar.....124
Brandy Hard Sauce..............180

Braun . 15, 25, 61, 107, 121, 179
Braun en Peurade................126
Braun Pye 61
Bread.....23, 25, 27, 31, 92, 108,
 114, 116, 120, 152, 158
Breadcrumbs..........................45
Brie Tart.................................72
Brussels sprouts.....................19
Butterd Worts.........................92
Buttered Marrows..................91
Cabbage..............19, 24, 80, 92
Cabbage in Broth...................80
Caboches in Potage 80
Camping....................27, 28, 31
Caraway.................................53
Carrots...............19, 78, 91, 113
Cauliflower 19
Chardewardon 76
Cheese.....21, 23, 24, 28, 31, 69,
 85, 95, 97, 98, 99, 137, 191
Cherries 20
Chicken ...19, 23, 25, 27, 33, 37,
 63, 64, 66, 80, 82, 95, 104,
 105, 107, 108, 109, 111, 113,
 116, 135
Chicken & Pork Hash...........130
Chickpea................................20
Chike Endored 105
Chives 39
Chocolate...............................31
Cinnamon........................21, 52
Civé de Veel.........................128
Coffee....................................22
Coffins..... 15, 25, 27, 47, 64, 66,
 67, 158
Colby......................................21
Collett & Alessandro's Wedding

Index

.... *170*

Conejas *111*

Contributors
   Anahita *17, 113, 116*
   Caellyn FitzHugh 47, 61, 66, 107
   Cariadoc *28*
   Cariadoc of the Bow *90, 117, 142, 158*
   Cariadoc of the Bow *17, 99*
   Cordelia Toser ... 55, 74, 98, 102, 130, 132, 139, 140, 144, 145, 159
   Elizabeth of Dendermonde 17, 90, 99, 142, 158
   Gwyneth Felton ... 126, 146, 148, 181
   Jehanne de St. Brieuc 63, 64, 72, 82
   Katerine *51, 53, 58, 76, 172*
   Kay of Triastrium *131*
   Serena Holmes *126, 146, 148*
   Siobhan fidhleir 69, 79, 80, 92
   Siobhan Medhbh .. 50, 52, 54, 57, 70, 77, 83, 85, 86, 87, 89, 91, 95, 97, 99, 104, 105, 108, 109, 118, 120, 123, 124, 128, 134, 135, 137, 151, 152, 155, 156, 160, 179

Cooler *27, 28, 111*

Cordials *144*

Coriander *53, 113, 117*

Cormarye *53*

Cornish game hens *38*

Crab apples *39*

Cranberries *20, 50*

Crème Boyled *150*

Cress in Lent with Milk of Almonds *85*

Cryspes *160*

Cubeb *21, 39, 82*

Cucumber *19*

Currants 20, 63, 66, 119, 120,
153

Custard Pudding *150*

Custard Tart *151*

Dairy Products *21*

Daryoles *151*

Dates *20*

Decorate .... See Presentation Issues

Desserts *146*

Dolmades *23*

Dolphin *37*

Dried Fruit Cordial *144*

Duck *19, 37, 54*

Eggplant *19*

Eggs .. 21, 24, 25, 33, 37, 63, 64, 66, 69, 72, 74, 95, 99, 113, 117, 151, 158

Emergencies *31*

Erbowle *155*

Estrella *32*

Feast for Christmas Day *164*

Firepits *31*

Fish .. 19, 23, 32, 54, 58, 85, 102

Fish Soup *140*

Food coloring *39, 105*

Food poisoning *30*

Food Tables *19*

Fresh Fruit Cordial *145*

Fried Cheese *97, 98*

Fruit Tarts *181*

Fruits *20, 39, 76*

Frumenty *89*

Funges *24, 82*

Funnel Cake *160*

Garleck Sawse *57*

Garlek Cameline *52*

Garlic 19, 24, 53, 54, 57, 58, 78, 87, 104

Gatorade *31*

Golden Rivers Anniversary

Fruit Tarts   Traveling Dysshes

Feast 2000.........................167	Minimal Cook Foods 24
Goose 19, 37, 54, 55, 104	Monterey Jack.......................21
Grains 19	Mortrews Blank 130
Grapes....20, 23, 39, 49, 63, 104	Mushrooms 19, 23, 24, 82
Great Pye 15	Mustard...............19, 67, 78, 92
Green Broth of Eggs & Cheese	Mustard Greens 90
....137	Mutton........................See Lamb
Green Egg & Cheese Soup...137	New World..............................16
Greens.........................78,83, 92	No Cook Choices 23
Greens & Beet Salad..............83	Old World 16
Grete Pye 64	Onions.. 24, 80, 87, 92, 114, 139
Guinea hen..............................37	Onions on Toast....................135
Ham..............23, 25, 27, 66, 121	Orange-Butter Sauce 157
Hard Sauce..............................15	Oranges..............................20, 31
Heat stress...............................31	Oxymel 142
Hedgehogs.....................24, 118	Parsnips 19, 39
Hotchpot de Poullaine 108	Pâté...23
Hypothermia 31	Peaches...................................20
Ice chest ....See cooler	Pears... 20, 25, 39, 76, 104, 146,
Jam Tarts 181	158
Jance Sawse 54	Pears in Wine Syrup 146
Lamb 19, 51, 113, 119	Peas..................................20, 24
Lasagne...................................95	Pennsic.............................28, 32
Leeks 19, 78, 80, 82, 92	Per Fare Tortiglione Ripieno
Legumes 20	152
Lemons...............................20, 39	Pevorade Sauce 24
Lentil 20	Pheasant 37
Lettuce.......................19, 78, 99	Pies 27, 61, 63, 66, 158, 159,
Longe Frutours 98	181
Loseyns...................................95	tarts................. 25, 69, 151, 181
Lovage....................................39	Pine nuts 20
Mail Order 34	Pineapples..............................20
Marrows.................................91	Piper Sauce.............................55
Mead 17, 22, 142	Plum.......................................20
Meatball Apples 132	Plum Pudding 155
Meats and Poultry..................19	Pork... 19, 25, 37, 48, 51, 53, 57,
Melons....................................20	61, 64, 67, 91, 92, 119, 121,
Menus....................................164	124, 126, 130, 132, 134, 179
Milk........21, 22, 47, 57, 89, 113	Potato.....................................19
Mincemeat Tart...............15, 180	Poumes.................................132

Traveling Dysshes   Fruit Tarts

Index

163

Powder douce............................42
Powder forte.............................43
Presentation Issues ..47, 48, 153
Prune.......................................20
Pudding..................................162
Pyes of Chiken..........................63
Pygge in a Coffin 66
Quail 37
Quaking Pudding.....................156
Quinces 104
Rabbit...........19, 33, 37, 51, 111
Radish 19
Raisins20, 51, 63, 120, 153, 158
Rape Armate............................79
Raspberry.................................20
Recipes Removed 179
References...............................172
Refrigeration............................28
Roast Pork....................124, 179
Roo Broth...............................134
Root beer.................................22
Rutabagas 19, 39
Saffron.....21, 39, 57, 58, 64, 80,
    82, 89, 105, 120, 146, 158
Sage Sauce 15, 50
Salad...............23, 24, 28, 78, 83
Salat 24, 78
Sallet of Beets, Currants &
    Greens...............................83
Salmon............................24, 102
Salmon Roste in Sauce.........102
Salomene...............................140
Sample Menus.......................167
Sauce 24, 25, 52, 53, 54, 55,
    57, 58, 76, 126
Sauces 27, 50, 51
Saunders..................................39
Sausage 23, 24, 25, 37, 118, 119
Sawse Cameline 51
Sawse Gauncile.......................57

Sawse Madam.......................104
SCA Merchants......................32
Scallion 19, 39
Scottish Night Feast at
    Collegium Occidentalis....169
Sekanjabin.....................22, 142
Shellfish...................................19
Shopping.......................32, 117
Shortbread...............................24
Soup 137
Soups............................27, 134
Sources...................................172
Sowpys Dorre.........................135
Spices 21, 27, 32, 33, 39, 80,
    119
Spinach ...15, 19, 70, 74, 78, 85,
    92, 99, 139, 181
Spinach Pie 74
Spinage Tart....................15, 181
Springform pans..15, 48, 62, 64,
    66, 67
Squash.....................................19
Steaks....................................131
Steamed Suet Pudding 162
Stekys of Venson or Bef........131
Stew..................24, 25, 113, 128
Stewed Beeff.........................120
Stews.......................................27
St7ilton...........................21, 191
Strawberries............................20
Strawberry Pudding.............148
Strawberye............................148
Strong powder.................42, 43
Stuffed Beef Rolls.................123
Stuffed Chicken....................109
Stuffed Tubes..........................97
Substitutions...........................37
Summer savory.......................39
Swan.................................19, 37
Sweet Fried Dough.............160

Fruit Tarts

Traveling Dysshes

Tabouli 23
Tart de Bry 72
Tartes of Spinage 70
Tea 22
To make a tarte of Spinnage .. 74
To Make Raspberry Wine 145
To Make The Surfit Water 144
Tomato 19
Tuna 37
Turkey 19
Turnip 78, 79, 85, 92
turnips 79, 120
Turnips 19, 39, 144
Twelfth Night Feast for the
   American Recorder Society
   168
Two Chikens from One 109
Vanilla 21
Veal 19, 33, 37, 51, 55, 128, 132
Veal Stew 128
Vegetables 19, 28, 78
Vegetarians ... 17, 23, 69, 80, 82,
   85, 92, 113, 116, 135, 137
Venison 19, 24, 25, 32, 33, 37,
   55, 64, 134

Venison or Beef Steaks 131
Verde Sawse 58
Verjuice 21, 27, 49, 54, 108
Viaunde of Cypres Ryalle 107
Vinegar ... 21, 39, 40, 50, 51, 52,
   53, 58, 78, 83, 86, 90, 102,
   104, 113, 120, 146, 170
Walnuts 51
Wardonys in Syryp 146
Watercress 85
Wheat Berries 89
White Sauce 57
White Tharidah of Al-Rashid .....
   113
Wine .. 17, 21, 22, 37, 39, 53, 63,
   67, 76, 77, 104, 108, 111,
   120, 121, 140, 142, 144, 146
Winter savory 39
Yam 19
Yeast Cake Stuffed with Raisins
   152
Yogurt 21
Yrchouns 24, 118
Zucchini 19, 91

Traveling Dysshes

Fruit Tarts

Notes

Notes

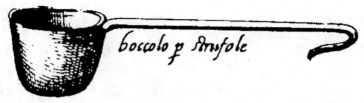

a Ladle

Endnotes

[1] UC Santa Cruz *CurrentsOnline*, 4 Feb 2002, http://www.ucsc.edu/currents/01-02/02-04/milk.html

[2] Cheddar cheese has an honorable history: "Cheddar was generally a peaceful agricultural village and thrived during the prosperous years of the 13th century, when its cheese was already famous." Cheddar Gorge official History, http://www.cheddarsomerset.co.uk/History/Cheddar%20History.htm

[3]

[4] "1872 -- Cream cheese is invented. In 1880, Philadelphia Cream Cheese was started, and in 1920, Breakstone Cream Cheese" Philadelphia Cream Cheese history, Kraft Foods company, http://www.kraft.com/archives/brands/brands_cream.html

[5] "Stilton is still made in much the same way as it was when Daniel Defoe, writing in his "Tour through England & Wales" in 1727, remarked that he "...passed through Stilton, a town famous for cheese". And yet, Stilton was never made in the town of Stilton! Stilton is situated about 80 miles north of London on the old Great North Road. In the 18th century, the town was a staging post for coaches traveling from London to York. Horses would be changed and travelers served light refreshments at one of the hostelries in the town. Cooper Thornhill, an East Midlands entrepreneur, was landlord at the famous Bell Inn and it was he who introduced these travelers to a soft, creamy, blue veined cheese which subsequently took its name from the town. Thornhill had brought the cheese from a farmer's wife by the name of Frances Pawlett who lived near Melton Mowbray." The Licensed Stilton Cheese Company, http://www.stiltoncheese.com/us.html

[6] I use Ziploc, Glad, or Hefty freezer-weight bags by preference, rather than the generics, if I really want to be sure the stuff in them doesn't leak all over the cooler. (smor)

Fruit Tarts   Traveling Dysshes